505
MOVIE
QUESTIONS
YOUR FRIENDS
CAN'T ANSWER

Other books in this series:

505 Baseball Questions Your Friends Can't Answer
(updated and revised)
John Kingston

505 Football Questions Your Friends Can't Answer
(updated and revised)
Harold Rosenthal

505 Hockey Questions Your Friends Can't Answer
Frank Polnaszek

505 Basketball Questions Your Friends Can't Answer
Sol Barzman

505 Boxing Questions Your Friends Can't Answer
Bert Sugar and John Grasso

and also:

505 Rock 'n' Roll Questions Your Friends Can't Answer
Nicholas and Elizabeth Schaffner

505 Theatre Questions Your Friends Can't Answer
John Beaufort

505 MOVIE QUESTIONS
YOUR FRIENDS CAN'T ANSWER

LOUIS PHILLIPS

 WALKER AND COMPANY
NEW YORK

This book is dedicated
with much affection to

CHARLES HUNT
and
IVY FISCHER-STONE

and with most grateful acknowledgement to: Michael Karp for
generously sharing his copious film knowledge, especially for
his Laurel and Hardy and Buster Keaton quizzes. A thank you
to the School of Visual Arts Library and to Sam Stetner for
sharing with me his film books.

First published in the United States of America in 1983 by the Walker Pub-
lishing Company, Inc.

Published simultaneously in Canada by John Wiley & Sons Canada, Limited,
Rexdale, Ontario.

ISBN: 0-8027-0717-3 Cloth
       0-8027-7199-8 Paper

Library of Congress Catalog Card Number: 82-42528

Printed in the United States of America

10 9 8 7 6 5 4 3 2 1

Contents

CONTENTS

FADE IN

General Quiz #1

1. Can you identify Fred Ott?

2. On September 15th of every year, William Holden used to send Barbara Stanwyck red roses. Why?

3. In Hong Kong, the title of the 1955 film was *The Heart of a Lady as Pure as a Full Moon Over the Place of Medical Salvation.* In the United States, the film was known by what shorter title?

4. When Vittorio De Sica approached David Selznick to raise money for *The Bicycle Thief* (1949), Selznick offered financing provided what movie star played the starring role of Antonio Ricci?

5. What was the first film shot in Hollywood, California?

6. Vilaiwan Seeboonreaung, Ngamta Suphaphongs, Javanart Punynchoti, and Kannikar Wowklee all receive screen credit for what major film of the 1950s?

7. Orson Welles's *The Magnificent Ambersons* (1942), François Truffaut's *Fahrenheit 451,* Tony Richardson's *Hamlet* (1969), and Robert Altman's *M*A*S*H* have what device in common?

8. In the summer of 1922, what future film great worked as a stilt-walker at Steeplechase Park in Coney Island?

9. In 1939 the United States Treasury reported that a certain film star was the nation's top wage earner. Who was the star? What did the star earn in 1939?

10. In 1915 some madly inventive moviemaker decided to film a silent movie version of the opera *Carmen,* using

members of the Metropolitan Opera Company. Who "sings" Carmen—even though she cannot be heard?

11. What actor said of himself, "I have a face like the behind of an elephant"?

12. Boris Karloff, far better known for his horror roles, plays an Indian—Guyasuta, Chief of the Senecas—in what 1947 film that starred Gary Cooper?

13. In the film version of *The Wizard of Oz*, what is Dorothy's last name?

14. What Los Angeles Dodger baseball star can be seen as an extra in the film *The Godfather, Part II* (1974)?

15. In the films *Dive Bomber, Navy Blues, One Foot in Heaven, They Died With Their Boots On,* and *The Male Animal,* there is an actor who appears under the name Bryant Fleming. By what name is he better known?

16. In 1948, how much did a movie extra get paid per day?

17. Although Lewis Stone is identified with the role of Judge Hardy in the Andy Hardy films, what actor played Judge Hardy in the very first film of that series?

18. We all know who Hedy Lamarr is, but who is Hedley Lamarr?

19. In 1934 Pioneer Pictures presented "the first full-length production filmed in glorious beauty of the New Technicolor. . . . The story of a glorious temptress who lived in luxury on nothing a year. . . . One of the most astonishing private lives in the annals of the world." Can you identify the film? The future wife of a United States President had a walk-on in that film. Who is she?

20. Who created the famous MGM slogan, "More stars than there are in heaven"?

ANSWERS

1. *Fred Ott can be called the first movie performer in America. He can be seen sneezing in the first American film, Edison's* Kineto-scope Record of a Sneeze. *The film was directed by W. K. L. Dickson, one of Edison's assistants.*

2. *It was Bill Holden's way of thanking her for the great help and encouragement she had given him during his first important film,* olden Boy. *The film opened at New York City's Radio City Music Hall on September 15, 1939.*

3. Not as a Stranger.

4. *Selznick wanted Cary Grant to play the starring role, but it went instead to Lamberto Maggiorani. The film went on to become a landmark of neo-realism.*

5. *D. W. Griffith's* In Old California *(1910) is often given credit for being the first film shot in Hollywood, California. The film features an actor named Frank Grandin. Mr. Grandin went on to become governor of California.*

6. *The names may be hard to pronounce, but they all receive credit for playing Siamese girls in* The Bridge on the River Kwai.

7. *The credits for each of these films is spoken, not spelled out.*

8. *Cary Grant. He received much of his stilt-walking training from Bob Pender's Troupe. (Cary Grant first ran away from home at age thirteen to try to join that troupe of actors and acrobats.)*

9. *Gary Cooper. In 1939, he earned $482,819. Money went much further in those days.*

10. *Geraldine Farrar sings the part of Carmen in what must have been one of the greatest exercises in futility of all time. No wonder Charlie Chaplin did a burlesque version of* Carmen.

[5]

11. *Charles Laughton. He was probably right.*

12. *Boris Karloff can be seen as a Seneca Chief in* Unconquered.

13. *In the film credits, the part is listed as "Dorothy Gale."*

14. *Steve Garvey.*

15. *Bryant Fleming was the film name first used by Gig Young.*

16. *In 1948 a movie extra received $15.56 for a day's work.*

17. *Lionel Barrymore was the first actor to play Judge Hardy on the screen.*

18 *Hedley Lamarr is the name of the character played by Harvey Korman in Mel Brooks's parody,* Blazing Saddles.

19. *Becky Sharp (based on* Vanity Fair*) was the first full-length production filmed in glorious technicolor. Pat Nixon has a walk-on in that film.*

20. *Howard Dietz, who was MGM's publicity chief in New York City, counted the stars in heaven and on MGM's lot.*

Lines of Dialogue

1. In what 1940 film does Humphrey Bogart say, "By the time I get home to my wife, I'll be too tired to turn out the light"?

2. "I'm trying to write good literature, but it always comes out nightingales and roses." That line is delivered in a film that is the biography of what world-famous dancer?

3. "When you call me that, smile!" That line has been delivered in quite a few westerns. What was the first western to bring that phrase to light?

4. Mayor (played by Harry Morgan): She takes after her dear departed mother.
   Sheriff (played by James Garner): Her mother is dead?
   Mayor: No. She just departed.
   The above lines occur in what 1969 comedy?

5. In his film debut in *The Devil's Run* (1975), this actor spoke only one line: "Blasphemer! Get him; he is a blasphemer!" The actor went on to greater things. Who is he?

6. He: I shot him in the stomach.
   She: Is he upset?
   In what film does that above exchange occur? Who plays the male lead? The female lead?

7. "In the twentieth century, the main product of all human endeavor is waste" is a line delivered by Orson Welles in a 1968 British comedy. Can you identify this film, in which Welles plays an advertising big shot?

8. "Ya know the trouble with you, Harry? You're just not

couth." This line is directed at Harry Brock in what film? Who plays Harry? Who delivers the line?

9. "You have the touch of a sex-starved cobra" is a line that can be heard in what classic film comedy?

10. Margo: . . . funny business, a woman's career. The things you drop on your way up the ladder, so you can move faster. You forget you'll need them again when you go back to being a woman.
    That line is from what great film?

11. "When you told me that you loved me, I was so proud I could have walked into a den of lions; in fact, I did, and the lions didn't hurt me." Bette Davis delivers that line in what 1942 film that takes its title from lines by Walt Whitman?

12. In what movie does Jimmy Stewart deliver the following line: "Every family has curious little traits. What of it? My father raises orchids at ten thousand dollars a bulb. Is that sensible? My mother believes in spiritualism. That's just as bad as your mother writing plays, isn't it?"

13. In what film will you hear the line: "Did you like that, Mama? I'm glad. I'd rather please you than anybody I know of"?

14. Who says, "You know how to whistle, don't you, Steve?" In what film?

15. "Just head for that big star; it will take us home" is the final line to what film?

ANSWERS

1. They Drive by Night.

2. *The line of dialogue is from* The Loves of Isadora *(1969), the biopic of Isadora Duncan. Vanessa Redgrave played the dancer, and James Fox played Gordon Craig.*

3. *That line comes from the Owen Wister novel* The Virginian. *In the 1929 film* The Virginian, *that line (as delivered by Gary Cooper) is: "If you want to call me that, smile."*

4. Support Your Local Sheriff.

5. *John Travolta.*

6. Badlands, *a Terrence Malik film that stars Martin Sheen and Terrence Malik, contains that black-comedic exchange.*

7. *The film is* I'll Never Forget Whatshisname.

8. *The line is from* Born Yesterday. *Judy Holliday delivers it to Broderick Crawford.*

9. *That line is delivered in* The Man Who Came to Dinner.

10. *The line is spoken by Margo Channing (as portrayed by Bette Davis) in the Joseph L. Mankiewicz film* All About Eve *(1950).*

11. Now Voyager. *In* Leaves of Grass, *Whitman wrote:*
    The untold want by life and land ne'er granted,
    Now voyager sail thou forth to seek and find.

12. You Can't Take It with You *(1938).*

13. *Al Jolson speaks that in* The Jazz Singer *(1927) after the first chorus of* Blue Skies. *This was the sound film that changed the course of motion picture history.*

14. *If you missed this one, hang your head in shame. That line, of course, is delivered by Lauren Bacall to Bogart in* To Have and Have Not.

15. The Misfits *(1961). This was the last line in the last Clark Gable movie. The script was written by Arthur Miller for his wife Marilyn Monroe. It was her final film also.*

Movie Ads

1. "X was never like this.
   X has never been known for its elegance. Or for its beautiful people, for its intelligent story lines, or for its brilliant photography.
   X has been known for other things.
   This movie has changed the meaning of X. It's the first film of its kind that makes you feel good without feeling bad."
   The above was an ad for what well-known X-rated film?

2. The ads for a certain film starring Charlton Heston and Edward G. Robinson said, "People need it . . . in the year————." What do the people need? In what year do they need it?

3. "Something hit us . . . the crew is dead . . . help us, please, please help us!" should make you think of what film?

4. Singing star Frankie Avalon can be seen in what Ray Milland film that was advertised as "an orgy of looting and lust"?

5. "Hell, upside down" should bring to mind what film?

6. Many film historians cite the line "Gable's back and Garson's got him" as the most famous advertising slogan in film history. What was the name of the MGM film it promoted?

7. "England had its Amber . . . America had its Scarlett . . . But you'll never forget the woman of Spain—marked forever as 'That Lady.'" *That Lady* introduced to the screen a noted English actor, an actor who would win an

Academy Award in 1966. Who is he? In the ad, who is Amber (we all know who Scarlett is).

8. The advertising posters for what film boasted of the following?: "Three years in research. 9,753 players in one scene alone! Sixteen Cinemascope color cameras. Filmed in Egypt by the largest location crew ever sent abroad from Hollywood! Its story from the Nobel Prize and Pulitzer Prize pen of William Faulkner."

9. In France the title of this Cary Grant film was advertised as *Grand Méchant Loup Appelle* ("Big Bad Wolf is Calling"). By what title is the film known in the United States?

10. Newspaper ads for the 1955 film *The Prodigal* read: "This is the story of the Prodigal Son who left his father's house for the fleshpots of sin-ridden Damascus! MGM's mighty love-drama. . . . Spectacularly presented! The biggest picture ever filmed in Hollywood! Two years in the making! A fortune to produce. . . . Woman's beauty and Man's temptation in the city of Sin." Who played the male lead? Who supplied the beauty and temptation? Who directed the film?

11. The ads proclaimed: "The Bank Robbery that caught a town with its morals down." The film starred Victor Mature, Richard Egan, Stephan McNally, Sylvia Sidney, J. Carroll Naish, and Ernest Borgnine. Can you identify this (far from major) film?

12. "Garbo Talks"—those two words from a 1930 MGM advertising campaign had filmgoers flocking to the theaters. What film introduced Garbo's speaking voice?

13. "Garbo Laughs"—those two words from a 1939 MGM advertising campaign had filmgoers running to the movie theaters once again. What film gave us Garbo's laughter?

14. "They're young. They're in love. And they kill people." That famous line is associated with what film?

15. What 1913 film (remade in 1925 and 1951) was hailed as a masterpiece by the great sculptor Rodin and was advertised as having a cast of five thousand people and thirty lions?

16. "Five great stars challenge you to guess the disguise roles they play!" To what John Huston film does that advertising gimmick refer? What five stars played the film in disguise and then peeled off their disguises at the end?

17. What five-million-dollar epic was advertised as being "the mightiest story of truth and temptation ever produced!" (Hint: This film introduced Paul Newman to the screen.)

18. The ads said: "You're headed in the right direction if you're *Arizona Bound*." That 1927 film provided the first starring role for what film great?

19. "Don't say it! See it!" That was the slogan for what Judy Holliday film?

20. Joel McCrea and Fay Wray star in a film that tells "the strange and startling story of a boy and a girl cast upon a jungle isle only to fall into the hands of a fascinating, though dangerous fiend who hunted men like beasts." What is the film?

21. What film (starring Clark Gable and Norma Shearer) was advertised with the slogan, "The film in which you hear the characters think"?

22. "Love means never having to say you're sorry" is a line associated with what film?

ANSWERS

1. Emmanuelle.

2. Soylent Green, *needed in the year 2022. This was Edward G. Robinson's last film.*

3. Airport *(1975). "An all new motion picture event—inspired by the novel* Airport *by Arthur Hailey."* Airplane *(1981), of course, was the hilarious spoof of the entire series of airplane disaster films.*

4. Panic in the Year Zero. *Ray Milland not only acted in the film, but he also directed it.*

5. The Poseidon Adventure.

6. Adventure.

7. *Paul Scofield, who won the 1966 Academy Award as best actor for his performance in* A Man for All Seasons. *Amber refers to the Kathleen Winsor novel* Forever Amber. *At one time the book was considered quite shocking.*

8. *Howard Hawks's* Land of the Pharaohs. *Harry Kunitz and Harold Jack Bloom also had a hand in the script. Sixteen hundred camels and 104 specially built barges were also frequently mentioned by the public relations people.*

9. *The film is* Father Goose *(1964). How a film can go from goose to wolf in translation remains a mystery. The song "Pass Me By," with music by Cy Coleman and lyrics by Caroline Leigh, is sung in this film.*

10. *Edmund Purdom. Lana Turner. The film was directed by Richard Thorpe.*

11. Violent Saturday *(1955). It must be embarrassing to catch a town with its morals down.*

12. Anna Christie, *based on the O'Neill play, was Garbo's first talkie.*

13. Ninotchka *was Garbo's first comedy film.*

14. Bonnie and Clyde.

15. Quo Vadis, *but who stays around to count the lions?*

16. The List of Adrian Messenger *(1963). The stars who wear disguises in the film are: Tony Curtis, Burt Lancaster, Kirk Douglas, Frank Sinatra, and Robert Mitchum.*

17 The Silver Chalice. *Paul Newman plays Basil the Defender.*

18. *Gary Cooper. He plays The Cowboy, a role that set a pattern for his long career. Betty Jewel plays The Girl.* Arizona Bound *was directed by John Waters.*

19. Phfft! *Not only did people not say it; they did not see it. The title came from a word coined by columnist Walter Winchell, who explained that the word was the sound of a marriage going flat.*

20. The Most Dangerous Game *(1932). In Great Britain the film was released under the title* The Hounds of Zaroff.

21. Strange Interlude *(1932), based on the stage play by Eugene O'Neill.*

22. Love Story *(1970), based on the best-selling novel by Erich Segal.*

THE CAST

Elizabeth Taylor

1. Elizabeth Taylor has made ten films with Richard Burton (at last count). Can you name at least seven of their films?

2. For what roles did Elizabeth Taylor win her Academy Awards as Best Actress?

3. Can you name all of Elizabeth Taylor's husbands (ex-husbands)—as of 1982?

4. Elizabeth Taylor is listed as the producer of what film?

5. Elizabeth Taylor once said, "Doing this picture gripes the hell out of me. . . . It's too commercial, it's in bad taste. Everyone in it is crazy, mixed-up sick—except for the part Eddie plays." What film was she so disgusted with?

6. Which Elizabeth Taylor film takes its title from a portion of the alphabet?

7. In what film did Elizabeth Taylor make her screen debut?

8. In what films does Elizabeth Taylor play the following roles:
   Susanna Drake
   Catherine Holly
   Mrs. Flora Golforth
   Ruth Wiley

9. Ads for which Elizabeth Taylor film stated that no one would be seated during the last twenty minutes?

ANSWERS

1. *The ten Elizabeth Taylor/Richard Burton movies are:* Hammersmith Is Out *(1972),* Under Milkwood *(1971),* Boom *(1968),* Dr. Faustus *(1967),* The Taming of the Shrew *(1967),* The Comedians *(1967),* Who's Afraid of Virginia Woolf? *(1966),* The Sandpiper *(1965),* The VIP's *(1963), and* Cleopatra *(1962).*

2. *Ms. Taylor won her Oscars for her roles in* Butterfield 8 *(1960) and* Who's Afraid of Virginia Woolf? *(1966).*

3. *Elizabeth Taylor's ex-husbands:*
   Conrad Hilton, Jr.
   Michael Wilding
   Michael Todd
   Eddie Fisher
   Richard Burton (twice)
   John Warner

4. *Elizabeth Taylor received credit as producer for the 1967 film* The Taming of the Shrew.

5. *Ms. Taylor was discussing* Butterfield 8, *for which she received an Oscar for Best Actress. Her husband Eddie Fisher also had a part in that film.*

6. *Elizabeth Taylor plays Zee in the film* X, Y and Zee. *(Sometimes the film is called* Zee and Company.*)*

7. *Elizabeth Taylor's first film role was in the 1941 movie* There's One Born Every Minute. *In that film the ten-year-old Ms. Taylor sings a duet with Carl 'Alfalfa' Switzer of "Our Gang" comedy fame.*

8. *Elizabeth Taylor portrays Susanna Drake in* Raintree County *(1957), Catherine Holly in* Suddenly Last Summer *(1959), Mrs. Flora Golforth in* Boom *(1968), and Ruth Wiley in* Elephant Walk *(1954).*

9. *Moviegoers were not seated during the final twenty minutes of the 1973 film* Night Watch, *which was based upon the play by Lucille Fletcher.*

Gary Cooper

1. What was Gary Cooper's first released film?

2. Gary Cooper narrated, produced, and performed in what 1949 technicolor sports short for Warner Brothers?

3. In what movie was Gary Cooper replaced because his love scenes were so terrible?

4. Gary Cooper makes an unbilled guest appearance (along with Roy Rogers and Gene Autry) in which 1959 Bob Hope comedy?

5. What was Gary Cooper's first all-talking picture?

6. "Even while he held one woman in his arms, he held another in his memory." So read the ads for what 1933 Gary Cooper movie?

7. All told, Gary Cooper made ninety-two films. What was his final movie?

8. Gary Cooper plays Dr. Joseph Frail in what movie?

9. In 1956 Gary Cooper recorded his first record. He sang a song from one of his films. Which song did he record? From what film? Who wrote the song?

ANSWERS

1. *Gary Cooper was first seen on the screen in a 1925 silent film called* The Thundering Herd.

2. Snow Carnival. *Coop, of course, was an avid sportsman.*

3. *Gary Cooper's love scenes in* Children of Divorce *(1927) were so awful that he was replaced. The actor who replaced Coop did not perform much better, so Gary Cooper returned to the set and finished the picture.*

4. *Coop makes an unbilled guest appearance in* Alias Jesse James. *Jay Silverheels as Tonto and Fess Parker as Davy Crockett can also be seen in this comedy.*

5. *His first all-talking picture was* The Virginian, *based upon Owen Wister's novel. The film was released in 1929.*

6. *That was the advertising line for* One Sunday Afternoon. *Fay Wray is Coop's co-star. The film portrays a dentist named Bill Grimes who always felt he married the wrong girl.*

7. *Gary Cooper's final film was a suspense film directed by Michael Anderson:* The Naked Edge *(1961). The film was based on Max Ehrlich's novel* First Train to Babylon.

8. *Dr. Joseph Frail is a character in* The Hanging Tree *(1958).*

9. *Coop sang "Marry Me, Marry Me." The song is from the movie* Friendly Persuasion. *Music by Dimitri Tiomkin. The record may well be a collector's item.*

Lana Turner

1. In what film does Lana Turner make her first appearance as an unbilled extra?

2. Great tragedy entered Lana Turner's life on April 4, 1958, when her fourteen-year-old daughter fatally stabbed a man romantically linked with her mother. Who was the man?

3. In June 1971 Lana Turner made her stage debut in a ten-week tour of what play?

4. Lana Turner made her official debut in a film called *They Won't Forget.* This film, directed by Mervyn LeRoy, is based upon an actual murder case. Which one?

5. In 1957 Lana Turner played the role of Constance MacKenzie in what film?

6. Erich Von Stroheim, Jr. worked as an assistant director on what 1961 Bob Hope–Lana Turner comedy?

7. The advertising slogan for the film *Diane* stated, "Lana Turner dares the devil in *Diane.*" This 1956 film portrays "the most cultivated woman of the French Renaissance." Who was Diane?

8. In reviewing a Lana Turner movie, a critic for the *New York Times* wrote: "Frankly, she is no more convincing as the drunken extra than she is as the star. She is an actress playing an actress, and neither one is real. A howling act in a wildly racing auto—pure bunk—is the top of her speed." Can you identify the film that the *Times* was referring to?

9. Lana Turner's real first name was not Lana. What was it?

ANSWERS

1. *Lana Turner is an extra in a racetrack sequence in the film* A Star Is Born *(1937). That film stars Janet Gaynor and Frederick March. Another actress, Carole Landis, is also an extra in the same scene.*

2. *Cheryl Crane stabbed Johnny Stompanato. The final verdict in the trial was justifiable homicide. This was not the first time that violence had brought suffering to Ms. Turner's life. On December 15, 1930 Lana Turner's father, Virgil, was robbed and slain in San Francisco.*

3. *The play was* Forty Carats.

4. *The film is based upon the famous Leo Frank murder case. A Jew from the North was accused of killing a boy in Atlanta and was eventually lynched by a mob; later, the man was found innocent.*

5. *Lana Turner plays Constance MacKenzie in* Peyton Place. *She received an Academy Award nomination as Best Actress for her performance.*

6. *Erich Von Stroheim, Jr. was the assistant director on* Bachelor in Paradise.

7. *Diane was Diane de Poiters, the mistress of King Henry II of France.*

8. *The* New York Times *critic attacked Lana Turner's performance in the 1953 film* The Bad and the Beautiful, *directed by Vincente Minnelli.*

9. *Her real first name was Julia.*

Marlene Dietrich

1. What was Marlene Dietrich's real name, and how did it inspire her screen name?

2. What Marlene Dietrich film was originally named *Chuck-a-Luck*?

3. For Alfred Hitchcock's film *Stage Fright*, Cole Porter wrote a song for Ms. Dietrich. What was it?

4. What was Dietrich's first film made in America?

5. In what movie does Marlene Dietrich wear a gorilla suit?

6. In what movie does Ms. Dietrich play a character named X-27?

7. The Harold Arlen and E. Y. Harburg songs "Willow in the Wind" and "Tell Me, Tell Me, Evening Star" are sung by Ms. Dietrich in which of her films?

8. Before Marlene Dietrich made *Song of Songs*, the film had already been made twice. What great silent film actresses had played the role of Lily before Ms. Dietrich did?

9. Famous novelist John Dos Passos was the screenwriter (along with S. K. Winston) for what 1935 Dietrich film?

10. In 1962 Marlene Dietrich provided the narration for what feature-length documentary that won the Academy Award for Best Documentary?

ANSWERS

1. *Her given name was Maria Magdalene. Marlene comes from the first half of Maria and the last part of Magdalene.*

2. *Rancho Notorious (1952) was originally titled Chuck-a-Luck because that phrase was a key to the film's plot. "The Legend of Chuck-a-Luck" was sung by William Lee for the film.*

3. *Cole Porter wrote "The Laziest Girl in Town" for Ms. Dietrich to sing in Stage Fright (1950).*

4. *Morocco (1930) was Ms. Dietrich's first American film. She played Amy Jolly, and Gary Cooper played Tom Brown. The film was based upon the novel Amy Jolly by Benno Vigny.*

5. *Blonde Venus (1932). For a singing number, Ms. Dietrich enters in a gorilla suit. She removes the head, puts on a blonde wig, and sings "Hot Voodoo."*

6. *X-27 is a spy in Dishonored (1931). Ms. Dietrich plays opposite Victor McLaglen.*

7. *The Arlen-Harburg songs are in the 1944 MGM production of Kismet.*

8. *Elsie Ferguson and Pola Negri play the role of Lily in earlier versions of Song of Songs.*

9. *The Devil Is a Woman (1935). The film was based upon Pierre Long's novel The Woman and the Puppet.*

10. *The Black Fox, an American documentary about Adolf Hitler. Caricatures by George Grosz can be seen in this film, along with some of Gustav Dore's illustrations for Dante's Inferno.*

John Wayne

1. How did John Wayne get his nickname "Duke"?

2. What great cowboy star gave John Wayne his first movie job?

3. What John Wayne western was originally shot in 3-D?

4. In 1950 Howard Hughes began a movie starring John Wayne and Janet Leigh. The film was not released until seven years later. What film took so long to complete?

5. Can you name two films directed by John Wayne?

6. Below is a list of some characters portrayed by John Wayne. Can you give the titles of the films in which these characters appeared?
   a. Thomas Dunson
   b. Sergeant John M. Stryker
   c. Dan Roman
   d. Roy Glennister

7. In *The Greatest Story Ever Told* (1965), what part does John Wayne play?

8. For what roles was John Wayne nominated for an Academy Award as Best Actor?

9. What was the first film produced by John Wayne?

ANSWERS

1. *When John was a child (and when his name was Marion Michael Morrison), his family had a large dog named Duke. Marion and the dog were always seen together, so people started referring to them as Big Duke and Little Duke.*

2. *Tom Mix hired Marion Morrison to move props and furniture on and off movie sets. The salary was $35.00 a week.*

3. *Hondo (1954), based upon a story by Louis L'Amour, was originally shot in the 3-D process, but it was released in a regular 35mm print format. The film was directed by John Farrow.*

4. *Jet Pilot, begun in 1950, was finally released in 1957. Through the years, Howard Hughes kept the actors running back and forth to shoot and reshoot key scenes.*

5. *John Wayne directed* The Alamo *(1960) and* The Green Berets *(1968).*

6. *a. Thomas Dunson*—Red River
    b. Sergeant Stryker—Sands of Iwo Jima
    c. Dan Roman—The High and the Mighty
    d. Roy Glennister—The Spoilers

7. *In George Stevens's biblical epic, John Wayne plays a centurion who leads Christ to be crucified.*

8. *He was nominated as best actor for his work in* Sands of Iwo Jima *and for* True Grit. *His role in* True Grit *brought him his only Oscar.*

9. *The first film produced by John Wayne was* The Angel and the Badman *(1947). The film was written and directed by James Edward Grant.*

Laurel and Hardy

1. What was the first picture in which Stan Laurel and Oliver Hardy appeared together? The first one in which they starred as a team?

2. Prior to their uniting as a team, Laurel did Hardy—and producer Hal Roach—a favor. What was it?

3. In 1939 Hardy was teamed with another comedian for one film. What is the film, who is the comedian, and why were they paired?

4. Before either of them entered films, Stan Laurel was understudy to another famous comedian. Who was he, and for what role was Laurel his understudy?

5. Oliver Hardy is famous for his "camera looks," in which he looks directly at the audience and registers disgust or frustration. Why were these looks sometimes expressions of how Hardy *really* felt?

6. What was Stan Laurel's real name?

7. Under what name was Oliver Hardy originally billed in his pre-Laurel-and-Hardy movies?

8. How did Oliver Hardy develop the characteristic gesture of fumbling with his tie?

9. The comedians found their last film very difficult work. What is the film, and why was it so hard to film?

10. What is the name of the well-known *Laurel and Hardy* theme song?

ANSWERS

1. Lucky Dog *(1917); Laurel is the star, Hardy appears briefly as a hold-up man. They first starred as a team in* Putting Pants on Philip *(1926).*

2. *Laurel substituted for Hardy in* Get 'Em Young *(1926) when Hardy, his hand scalded in a cooking accident, was unable to play the role.*

3. *Hardy plays opposite Harry Langdon in* Zenobia. *Throughout their careers with Hal Roach, Hardy and Laurel worked under separate contracts; Laurel's had expired a year earlier than Hardy's, hence the pairing for Hardy's last Roach-produced film.*

4. *While both were in Fred Karno's British Music Hall troupe, Laurel stood by as Charlie Chaplin's understudy in the revue,* A Night In an English Music Hall *(Chaplin starred as a drunken heckler in the theater box).*

5. *Often, Laurel would suggest waiting until the end of the day to photograph Hardy's exasperated expressions because by then, Hardy was dying to get to the golf course or track and would be annoyed at any further delay.*

6. *Arthur Stanley Jefferson.*

7. *"Babe" Hardy. The nickname was given to him by a barber in Florida who, while shaving Hardy, would croon, "That's a nice baby."*

8. *In a moment of on-camera confusion, Hardy was doused with a bucket of water. Starting to ad-lib by blowing his nose in his tie, he suddenly thought the gesture would be too vulgar, and the movement was transformed into an embarrassed "tie-twiddle".*

9. *Shot in Spain,* Atoll K *was directed by a director who spoke only Spanish, and starred Laurel and Hardy, who spoke only English. The rest of the cast spoke only Portuguese. More time was spent on communicating among the various parties than on actually shooting the film.*

10. *"The Dance of the Cuckoos."*

Buster Keaton

1. What was Keaton's real name? Who gave him the sobriquet "Buster," and why?

2. Fatty Arbuckle was Keaton's mentor in films. What was the last film Keaton and Arbuckle appeared in together?

3. Name and describe the vaudeville act that Keaton and his parents performed.

4. Although from a show-biz family, Keaton once seriously considered another career. What was that career?

5. One of Keaton's last films was written by a famous dramatist. Name the film and the author.

6. Name the first full-length feature in which Keaton starred.

7. What was Buster Keaton's first talking film? His last silent movie?

8. Buster Keaton hired a well-known character actor to direct the dramatic parts of one of his films. Name the actor and the film.

9. Two of Keaton's films take place almost entirely on a railroad. What are they?

10. Who was Keaton's partner in his early sound films?

11. In the late thirties through the forties, Keaton was employed as a "gag consultant" by MGM. Only one comedian at that studio successfully used Keaton's talents and, in fact, was the star of two films that were remakes of Keaton successes. Who was the comedian, and what were the films?

ANSWERS

1. *His real name was Joseph Keaton, Jr. As a child, he fell down the steps of a medicine show wagon while his parents were performing. Fellow performer Harry Houdini saw him take the fall and said, "That was some buster you took." The name stuck, and it was Buster Keaton from then on.*

2. The Round Up *(1920). As a throwaway gag, Keaton was dressed as an Indian and "shot" by Arbuckle. For this uncredited (and unrecognized) bit part, Keaton was paid a $7.50 stunt fee.*

3. *"The Three Keatons" was a rowdy knockabout act, in which Joe Keaton, Sr. threw his son around the stage and into the scenery while his mother, Myra, played the saxophone.*

4. *Civil engineer.*

5. *The film was* Film, *written by Samuel Beckett.*

6. The Saphead *(1920).*

7. Spite Marriage *(1930);* The Cameraman *(1929).*

8. *The director was Donald Crisp; the film,* The Navigator. *Much to Keaton's dismay, Crisp kept trying to inject comedy into the serious moments and would show up on the set with, in the comedian's words, "the damnedest gags you ever saw."*

9. The General *(1926) and* The Railroader *(1965), a Canadian Film Board travelogue.*

10. *Jimmy Durante.*

11. *Red Skelton was the comedian whose style was closest to Keaton's. Understandably, he starred in the films that had originally starred Keaton,* Marching through Georgia *(a remake of* The General) *and* Watch the Birdie *(originally* The Cameraman).

Joan Crawford

1. What was Joan Crawford's real name? How did she receive the name Joan Crawford?

2. What was the name of Joan Crawford's first husband? Her second husband?

3. In what film does Joan Crawford appear with Robert Young, Frank Lovejoy, and Eve Arden? Joan Crawford plays Agatha Reed, a congresswoman who returns to her alma mater to receive an honorary degree.

4. In 1926 Joan Crawford appeared in Harry Langdon's first full-length screen comedy, a story centering around Langdon's entrance into a cross-country hiking contest. What is the name of the comedy?

5. In a 1954 movie, Joan Crawford plays Vienna, a woman who manages a gambling saloon in Arizona. What is the name of this western?

6. In 1962 Joan Crawford appeared with Bette Davis and Victor Buono in a film about a former child star and her sister. What is the title of this classic horror film?

7. In *Lady of the Night* (1925), Joan Crawford acts as the double for what well-known actress?

8. Who is Billie Cassin?

9. Although Faye Dunaway plays the part of Joan Crawford in the movie *Mommie Dearest* (1981), she was not the first choice for the role. Who turned down the role?

10. In 1968 Joan Crawford was called upon to replace an actress in the TV soap opera *The Secret Storm*. Whom did Joan Crawford replace?

ANSWERS

1. *Joan Crawford's real name was Lucille Le Sueur. Did she change it because it sounded too much like a sewer? MGM sponsored a contest to find a new name for Ms. Le Sueur, and Marie M. Tisdale of Albany, New York submitted the name Joan Crawford.*

2. *Douglas Fairbanks, Jr. was her first husband. Franchot Tone was her second.*

3. Goodbye, My Fancy *(1951). The title of the film (and the hit play upon which it is based) comes from a poem by Walt Whitman.*

4. Tramp, Tramp, Tramp.

5. Johnny Guitar.

6. What Ever Happened to Baby Jane?

7. *Joan Crawford doubled for Norma Shearer.*

8. *Billie Cassin was another name taken by Joan Crawford (Lucille Le Sueur) when she was young. She took on this identity when her mother married a vaudeville theater owner named Harry Cassin.*

9. *Anne Bancroft was originally selected to play Joan Crawford in* Mommie Dearest, *but she turned down the role. Faye Dunaway took the role and turned in a marvelous performance.*

10. *Joan Crawford replaced her adopted daughter, Christina— author of* Mommie Dearest—*on the soap opera* The Secret Storm.

Cary Grant

1. Everyone knows that Cary Grant's real name was Archibald Leach. But what was his middle name?

2. Throughout his long and distinguished career, Cary Grant never received an Academy Award for best actor. He was, however, nominated twice—for what roles in what films?

3. In 1970 Cary Grant received a special Academy Award. Who presented the Oscar to Cary?

4. The role of Mortimer Brewster in the film version of Joseph Kesserling's hit comedy *Arsenic and Old Lace* (1944) was not originally offered to Cary Grant. To what actor was the role originally offered?

5. When we think of Asta the dog, we think of the Thin Man series. But in what Cary Grant film does a marital dispute arise over ownership of a dog named Asta?

6. In 1946 Cary Grant made a guest appearance (unbilled) in what John Wayne/Claudette Colbert film?

7. Cary Grant made four films with Alfred Hitchcock. Can you name them?

8. What is the title of the first movie to give Cary Grant top billing?

9. Cary Grant's first wife plays opposite Charlie Chaplin in *City Lights.* What is her name?

10. In 1944 Cary Grant was featured in *Once Upon a Time,* a film about a young boy who owns a pet named Curly.

Curly dances to the young boy's music. What kind of animal is Curly?

11. In 1933 Cary Grant played the part of Captain Cummings, a man engaged in missionary work. He attempts to reform a Lady named Lou. What is the title of the film? Who plays Lady Lou?

12. Mickey Mantle, Roger Maris, Yogi Berra, and Art Passarella all appear in what 1962 Cary Grant/Doris Day film?

13. In 1939, newspaper ads for a Cary Grant film read: "It's worth championship prices for a ringside seat when these two girls get in there and fight for the man one tricked and the other doesn't trust. They're biting in the clinch, because Kay won't let him go without a scandal, and Carole won't take him without a wedding ring. . . . A romance that couldn't be more modern if it were made next year." What is the film's title? Who are Carole and Kay?

ANSWERS

1. *Alex. Archibald Alex Leach was born on January 18, 1904, to Elsie and Elias Leach.*

2. *He was nominated for the role of Roger Adams in* Penny Serenade *(1941), and for the role of Ernie Mott in* None But the Lonely Heart *(1944).*

3. *Frank Sinatra presented the award. The inscription on the special Academy Award read:*

> To Cary Grant
> For his unique mastery
> of the art of screen acting
> With the respect and affection
> of his colleagues

4. *The role was originally offered to Bob Hope.*

5. The Awful Truth *(1937). The film was remade in 1953 as* Let's Do It Again.

6. Without Reservation *(1946). Cary Grant can be seen dancing with Claudette Colbert.*

7. *The four films he made with Hitchcock are:*
Suspicion
Notorious
To Catch a Thief
North By Northwest

8. Gambling Ship *(1933).*

9. *His first wife was Virginia Cherrill.*

10. *The animal was a caterpillar. The title of the movie emphasizes its fairy-tale qualities.*

11. *The film is* She Done Him Wrong. *Mae West plays Lady Lou. The film was based upon Mae West's own stage success* Diamond L'il. *Paramount pictures was close to bankruptcy when they hired Ms. West to adapt her play. The film made $12,000,000 in three months. Cary Grant was already a known feature player by the time he made his appearance in* She Done Him Wrong, *and so Mae West's claim that she discovered him (supposedly by pointing him out and saying, "Get me him. If he can talk, I'll take him") reportedly made him angry.*

12. That Touch of Mink.

13. *The film is* In Name Only. *Starring with Cary Grant are Carole Lombard and Kay Francis.*

Clark Gable

1. Clark Gable and Joan Crawford appear in eight films together. Can you name four?

2. When Ed Sullivan held a newspaper contest in which fans were asked to name the king and queen of Hollywood, Clark Gable (of course) was named the king. Who was named the queen?

3. The walls of Jericho play an important role in what Gable movie?

4. The 1953 Clark Gable/Ava Gardner film *Mogambo* is basically a remake of what earlier Clark Gable hit?

5. In what movies does Clark Gable play the following characters: Harry Van, Gay Langland, and Commander "Rich" Richardson?

6. *Gone With the Wind* was nominated for (and received) many Academy Awards. Clark Gable, however, did not receive the Oscar for Best Actor (though Vivien Leigh received the Best Actress award). Who won the Academy Award for Best Actor the year that Gable was nominated for his role of Rhett Butler?

7. In 1924 Clark Gable appeared as an extra in his very first film. The film was directed by Ernst Lubitsch. What was the film?

8. In 1948 *Theatre Arts* wrote of this film, "Done almost exactly as on Broadway, ———— ———— emerges as an intelligent, gripping film. The only disappointment is Clark Gable, who in every way fails to match the stage performance. . . ." What film was being reviewed?

9. In 1954 Clark Gable formed his own film production company. He called it GABCO. What was the first film produced by GABCO?

ANSWERS

1. *Clark Gable and Joan Crawford appear in the following films:* Strange Cargo *(1940),* Love on the Run *(1936),* Chained *(1934),* Forsaking All Others *(1934),* Dancing Lady *(1933),* Possessed *(1931),* Laughing Sinners *(1931), and* Dance, Fools, Dance *(1931). The last-named film was the first in which they appeared together.*

2. *Myrna Loy was named the queen.*

3. *The "walls of Jericho" was the name humorously applied to the blanket that separated Clark Gable from Claudette Colbert in* It Happened One Night *(1934).*

4. Mogambo *is a remake of the 1932 MGM film* Red Dust. *Both films were based upon the stage play by Wilson Collison.*

5. *Clark Gable plays Harry Van in* Idiot's Delight, *Gay Langland in* The Misfits, *and Commander "Rich" Richardson in* Run Silent, Run Deep.

6. *Robert Donat beat out Gable that year for the Oscar. Donat was voted the award for his performance in* Good-bye, Mr. Chips.

7. *Clark Gable's first screen role was in* Forbidden Paradise, *a film starring Pola Negri and Rod La Rocque.*

8. *The 1948 film reviewed by* Theatre Arts *was* Command Decision.

9. *The first film GABCO produced (in association with other producers) was* The King and Four Queens *(1954), with Gable and Jo Van Fleet.*

FREEZE FRAME

General Quiz #2

1. Sometimes going to the movies can feel like a month in the country. The five films below all run over two hours. Can you arrange the list of films in order from the longest running time to the (relatively) shortest?
The Bridge on the River Kwai
Gone With the Wind
Cleopatra
Ben Hur (1959)
The Deer Hunter

2. What film did President Nixon screen in the White House before he announced the invasion of Cambodia?

3. General Eisenhower called it "the greatest war picture I've ever seen." The picture was directed by William Wellman and stars Burgess Meredith as World War II's most famous war correspondent. Can you identify the film and the main character?

4. Here's an easy one for a change. In the 1953 movie, *Abbott and Costello Go to Mars,* what planet do the comedians land on?

5. In the 1970s there was a rock group called Klaatu. From what science fiction classic did the music group take its name?

6. Barbara Harris plays a character named Albuquerque in what 1975 film?

7. Brody, Quint, Hooper, Ellen Brody, Vaughn Meadows, and an Interviewer are characters in what highly successful film?

8. Everyone has heard of the western star William S. Hart, but few people know what the S. stands for. Do you?

9. Who played Captain Marvel in the 1941 Republic serial *The Adventures of Captain Marvel*?

10. What well-known comedian appears in such films as *Run Silent, Run Deep* (1958), *X, The Man With the X-ray Eyes* (1960), *Muscle Beach Party* (1964), and *Kelley's Heroes* (1970)?

11. James Stewart stars in four Alfred Hitchcock films. Can you name them?

12. Jean Harlow died before this film was completed, and another actress was brought in to take her place. What was the name of the film, and what actress appears in the long shots?

13. The film opens by showing the audience a film crew setting up lights, cameras, and props in Lyme Bay, England. Then a clapper board appears in front of the camera. This is the opening of what film?

14. When they think of *Peter Pan,* filmgoers immediately think of Walt Disney's animated classic. But in 1924 a live action version of *Peter Pan* was screened. Who played Captain Hook in that version?

15. A character named Ezra Ounce, who is an eccentric millionaire in charge of the Ounce Society for the Elevation of American Morals can be seen in what 1934 film?

16. Jose Ferrer won a 1950 Academy Award for his Cyrano in *Cyrano De Bergerac,* but can you name the actress who played Roxanne?

17. When Greta Garbo made her first American film *The Torrent* (1926), who doubled for her in the riding sequences? (Hint: It was a man who would go on to become a leading star himself.)

18. Mercy Humppe, Polyester Poontang, Good Time Eddie Filth, The Presence, and Uncle Limelight are just some of the characters in what 1969 film directed by Anthony Newley?

19. Who was the hip-talking disc jockey who helped promote the Beatles during their first visit to the United States in 1964 and who can be seen in the second Beatles' film, *Help!* (1965)?

20. What movie actress was billed in ads as 'The Kissing Bug' of Andy Hardy?

ANSWERS

1. *The order, from longest running to shortest, is:*
Cleopatra *(243 minutes)*
Gone With the Wind *(220 minutes)*
Ben Hur *(1959) (212 minutes)*
The Deer Hunter *(183 minutes)*
The Bridge on the River Kwai *(161 minutes)*

2. Patton. *The film was screened by President Nixon more than once.*

3. The Story of GI Joe. *The correspondent is Ernie Pyle. Ernie Pyle has also been honored by having his portrait appear on a United States postage stamp.*

4. *In this film they land on Venus. Oh well, you can't win 'em all.*

5. *Klaatu is a character in* The Day the Earth Stood Still *(1951).*

6. Nashville, *directed by Robert Altman.*

7. *Those are the characters in* Jaws *(1975). Peter Benchley, who wrote the novel and co-authored the screenplay, can be seen as the interviewer.*

8. *S. stands for Surrey.*

9. *Tom Tyler. Films in the serial were directed by William Witney and John English.*

10. *Don Rickles.*

11. Rope *(1948);* Rear Window *(1954);* The Man Who Knew Too Much *(1956); and* Vertigo *(1958).*

12. *Jean Harlow died in a plane crash before she had finished making* Saratoga. *Mary Dees is the actress who stood in for the long shots so that the film could be completed.*

13. The French Lieutenant's Woman, *starring Meryl Streep.*

14. *Ernest Torrance played Captain Hook. The film starred Betty Bronson and Anna May Wong.*

15. Dames, *with Dick Powell and Ruby Keeler.*

16. *Mala Powers.*

17. *Joel McCrea.*

18. Can Heironymus Merkin Ever Forget Mercy Humppe and Find True Happiness?—*indeed one of the more memorable film titles of all time.*

19. *Murray Kaufman, alias Murray the K. He died in 1982 at age sixty. He often referred to himself as the "fifth Beatle."*

20. *Lana Turner.*

ON THE SILVER SCREEN (THE FILM GENRES)

Comedy

1. What noted comedian makes an uncredited appearance as George Schmidlapp in the film *Will Success Spoil Rock Hunter?* (1957)?

2. In 1958 a short film starring Bob Hope, Bing Crosby, Ernie Kovacs, Edie Adams, Groucho Marx, and Orson Bean was released to promote sales of a national magazine. What was the film? What magazine did the film promote?

3. In what American film comedy can viewers see Eucalyptus trees even though the film is set on the coast of Maine, where Eucalyptus trees do not grow?

4. In what Jerry Lewis film does Jerry play seven different roles?

5. When James Thurber's classic short story "The Secret Life of Walter Mitty" was transferred to the screen, who played Walter Mitty?

6. This film comedian owns a film production company named Black Rain, a company that takes its name from the comedian's daughter, who is named Rain. Who is this film star?

7. What film comedy was advertised with the following trio of limericks:
   There was a young gal named Claudette
   Who was pretty and sweet and in debt.
   　So she got an old honey
   　With plenty of money
   Which he hasn't got now, you can bet!

And there was a guy named McCrea
Who married Claudette one fine day.
   She sampled his kisses
   And said: "Dear, if this is
Your best, then I'm going away."

So Claudette up and took a big chance,
She said: "Florida's great for romance!"
   On the train, this cute missa
   Stepped right on the kisser
Of the richest young tightwad in pants.

8. What film actor of numerous comedies once said, "I was usually a leering villain, killed in the first reel. Fortunately, in 1936, Gregory La Cava decided I might do a phony artist, something between a gigolo and a dilettante, in his picture *My Man Godfrey*. That's when I hit the Hollywood mother lode. That one role made a comedian out of me."

9. We all know who King Kong is, but in what film is there a pilot named Major T. J. "King" Kong? Who plays the part?

10. What well-known comedienne has a bit part, playing nightclub hostess Texas Guinan, in the 1961 film *Splendor in the Grass*?

11. In what movie does Ernie Kovacs play Harry Foster Malone, "the meanest man in the world"?

12. Who were Al Joachim, Jimmy Joachim, and Harry Joachim?

13. What member of the Three Stooges can be seen playing the bartender in the 1940 W. C. Fields film *The Bank Dick*?

14. On October 9, 1973, what great film and television comic married Lothian Toland, the daughter of Gregg To-

land—the cameraman on *Citizen Kane* and many other films?

15. *Life* magazine said of this film comedian that his face was as "unforgettable as the Eiffel Tower; it has helped to make him his country's greatest comic attraction." Who is he?

16. What great film comedian made his final film appearance playing Smiler Grogan in Stanley Kramer's 1963 all-star comedy *It's a Mad, Mad, Mad, Mad World*?

ANSWERS

1. *Groucho Marx played George Schmidlapp. In England, the film was called* Oh! For a Man!

2. *The film was called* Showdown at Ulcer Creek. *Billed as "an adult eastern," the film was used to promote the* Saturday Evening Post.

3. The Russians Are Coming, The Russians Are Coming. *In that film the Eucalyptus trees are not the only mistake. In one scene a young girl is talking to a character played by John Philip Law, and the sweater she is wearing changes from one kind to another.*

4. *Jerry Lewis plays seven different roles in* The Family Jewels *(1965).*

5. *Danny Kaye, who was born David Daniel Kaminsky in Brooklyn, in 1913. When the Walter Mitty film was released, Danny Kaye revealed to a reporter a Mitty-like fantasy of his own, "I'd like to have Lauren Bacall whistle at me."*

6. *Richard Pryor owns the film production company named Black Rain, named after one of his daughters, Rain (who was born in 1969). He has two other daughters: Renee (born in 1957) and Elizabeth Ann (born in 1967).*

7. *Those limericks were used to promote the 1942 film* The Palm Beach Story, *directed by Preston Sturges. Fortunately, the limericks don't really reflect the quality of the film comedy.*

8. *Mischa Auer said that. He was known to some fans as "The Mad Russian." It is ironic that only several months after his last film—* Drop Dead, Darling—*he did indeed drop dead, of a heart attack on March 5, 1967.*

9. *Major T. J. "King" Kong was played by Slim Pickens in the classic American comedy* Dr. Strangelove, or How I Learned to Stop Worrying and Love the Bomb *(1963).*

10. *Phyllis Diller. She also makes an unbilled guest appearance in* The Sunshine Boys.

11. *Ernie Kovacs plays the meanest man in the world in the Doris Day film* It Happened to Jane. *The film is sometimes shown under the title* Twinkle and Shine.

12. *Al, Jimmy, and Harry were better known as the Ritz Brothers.*

13. *Shemp Howard. He can also be seen in a serious role in the 1943 film* Pittsburgh, *starring Marlene Dietrich, Randolph Scott, and John Wayne.*

14. *On October 9, 1973, Red Skelton married Lothian Toland, the daughter of cameraman Gregg Toland.*

15. *Fernandel. His real name was Fernand Joseph Désiré Contandin.*

16. *Jimmy Durante makes his last screen appearance in that film. In it, Smiler Grogan kicks the bucket, and we actually see his foot kicking the bucket.*

Mysteries/ Suspense

1. In what 1930 film can viewers see Philo Vance and Sherlock Holmes killed off by Dr. Fu Manchu?

2. François Truffaut has made two films adapted from the writings of Cornell Woolrich. Can you name them?

3. In *The Penguin Pool Murder* (1932), a schoolteacher who has brought her class to the aquarium discovers a corpse in a penguin tank. This detective is often noted for odd choice of hats. Can you identify the detective? Who plays her in this film? Who plays her in later films?

4. The 1936 film *Meet Nero Wolfe* was based upon what Rex Stout novel? Who played Nero Wolfe? Who played Archie Goodwin? In the 1937 film *The League of Frightened Men,* who played Nero Wolfe? Who played Archie Goodwin?

5. What fictional detective (known to readers as "The American Sherlock Holmes") made his first film appearance in a 1915 Pearl White serial, *The Exploits of Elaine*?

6. In 1963, what mystery writer portrayed a detective created by himself in a film?

7. In the 1940 Columbia serial *The Shadow,* who portrayed "The Shadow"?

8. George Segal plays Morris Brummell, a New York City detective who finally outwits Christopher Gill, a theatrical producer (played by Rod Steiger) who enjoys strangling women. What is the name of the film?

9. Who played Father Brown in the 1935 film *Father Brown, Detective?* When the film was remade in 1954, who played Father Brown?

10. Scottie Ferguson (played by James Stewart) is a retired San Francisco policeman who suffers from acriphobia. Can you identify the film?

11. At least seven actors have played the part of Raymond Chandler's hard-boiled detective Philip Marlowe. Can you name any four?

12. In 1922 John Barrymore played Sherlock Holmes on the screen. Who played Dr. Watson? Who plays Dr. Watson in the Basil Rathbone versions?

13. In *The Heat of the Night,* Sidney Poitier plays a homicide expert for Philadelphia's police force. What is the name of the homicide expert?

14. What world-famous entertainer played the role of Federal Agent Quentin Locke in *The Master Mystery?* (Hint: His real name was Erich Weiss.)

ANSWERS

1. *Philo Vance and Sherlock Holmes and Dr. Fu Manchu all appear together in a comedy skit sequence in* Paramount on Parade. *The skit made it possible for Paramount to show off three valuable screen properties at the same time.*

2. *François Truffaut made two films based on Cornell Woolrich's works:* The Bride Wore Black (La Mariée était en noir, *1967) and* The Mississippi Mermaid (La Sirène du Mississippi, *1969). The latter film was based on the book* Waltz into Darkness.

3. *The detective was Hildegarde Withers, as portrayed by Edna May Oliver. Helen Broderick and Zasu Pitts also play the role in other films. Eve Arden played Ms. Withers for a TV pilot, but the series did not get shot.*

4. *In* Meet Nero Wolfe, *Edward Arnold plays the detective and Lionel Stander plays Archie. The film was based upon the novel* Fer-de-Lance. The League of Frightened Men *gives viewers a Nero Wolfe as played by Walter Connolly. Lionel Stander once again plays Archie.*

5. *Craig Kennedy was known as the American Sherlock Holmes to many readers. Arnold Daly and Pearl White defeat the "Clutching Hand" in* The Exploits of Elaine *(1915). The Clutching Hand was later developed into a fifteen-chapter serial in 1936, with Jack Mulhall playing the detective.*

6. *Mickey Spillane portrays Mike Hammer in* The Girl Hunters. *(It's not often that authors get to portray their own creations.) Mickey Spillane can be seen playing himself in the film* Ring of Fear *(1954).*

7. *Victor Jory plays* The Shadow. *James Horne directed the fifteen-chapter serial. The Shadow was created by Walter B. Gibson, who wrote the stories under the name Maxwell Grant.*

8. No Way to Treat a Lady *(1968). One of the victims was no lady. "She" was played by female impersonator Kim August.*

9. *Walter Connolly played Father Brown in 1935. Alec Guinness stars in the 1954 film.*

10. *Alfred Hitchcock's* Vertigo.

11. *William Powell, Humphrey Bogart, Robert Montgomery, George Montgomery, James Garner, Elliott Gould, and Robert Mitchum.*

12. *Roland Young played Dr. Watson to Barrymore's Holmes. Nigel Bruce is perhaps the most famous Watson of them all; he was in both the films and the radio shows with Rathbone.*

13. *Virgil Tibbs is the name of the Sidney Poitier character. The character also appears in* They Call Me Mr. Tibbs *(1970) and in* The Organization *(1970).*

14. *Harry Houdini. The film was made sometime between 1910 and 1920.*

Science Fiction and Horror

1. The species of monster represented in the film *20,000,000 Miles to Earth* is for some strange reason identified as an Ymir. In Norse mythology, who is Ymir?

2. Weak Chin and King Lowbrow are characters in what 1914 silent film? Who play the roles? The film is a parody of what D. W. Griffith film?

3. The evil scientist Rotwang is an unforgettable character. In what sci-fi classic does he appear? Who plays Rotwang?

4. The 1956 sci-fi classic *Forbidden Planet* is loosely based upon what Shakespearean play?

5. What 1958 film made movie history (of a sort) by featuring an inflatable skeleton that slid out of the screen and then dangled momentarily over the heads of the movie audience?

6. In the 1930s, why did Adolf Hitler order the destruction of all available prints and models for Fritz Lang's film *Die Frau im Mond* (1928)?

7. In *The Bride of Frankenstein* (1935), Boris Karloff, of course, plays the Monster and Elsa Lanchester plays his bride. But in that film who played the role of Mary Shelley, the author of the classic novel *Frankenstein*?

8. Steve McQueen made his screen debut in what 1958 horror film?

9. The conflict between Eloi and Morlocks is important to what science-fiction film?

10. Music by Richard Strauss, Johann Strauss, Aram Khachaturian, and Gyorgy Ligeti can be heard on the soundtrack of what classic science fiction film?

11. The monster in *Frankenstein,* The Mummy, and Dr. Fu Manchu are all portrayed on the screen by Boris Karloff. What other screen star has also played those three roles?

12. What 1953 sci-fi movie was filmed in 3-D and deals with an amateur astronomer named John Putnam watching a spaceship land in the desert? The movie was based upon a treatment by what great sci-fi writer? Who directed the film? (Hint: The director can be seen as an actor in *Citizen Kane.*)

13. Where was Bela Lugosi born? (Once you know, you will have an easy time remembering.)

14. Who played The Creature—referred to as "The Gill Man"—in *The Creature From the Black Lagoon*?

15. The 1950 movie *Destination Moon* was based upon what 1947 novel by Robert A. Heinlein?

16. What actor plays The Thing in *The Thing from Another World* (1951)?

17. In what sci-fi film can audiences see three well-known radio and newspaper reporters: Drew Pearson, H. V. Kaltenborn, and Gabriel Heater?

18. In the film *Destroy All Monsters* a battle cry is put forth to destroy four of the most famous of all Japanese monster-creatures. Can you name them?

19. In 1942 *The Ghost of Frankenstein* was released. Boris Karloff, however, does not play the monster in this film. Who does?

ANSWERS

1. *Ymir is the giant from whose body the gods created the world. It would be ironic, then, for an Ymir to turn around and destroy the world.*

2. *The 1914 film is* His Prehistoric Past. *Charlie Chaplin plays Weak Chin. Mack Swain plays King Lowbrow. This Chaplin film, which is a parody of D. W. Griffith's* Man's Genesis, *is sometimes presented under the title* A Dream.

3. *The film is* Metropolis. *Klein Rogge plays the scientist. "We have made machines out of men," Rotwang declares. "Now I will make men out of machines—a robot indistinguishable from a real woman."*

4. *There are very close parallels between* Forbidden Planet *and William Shakespeare's* The Tempest. *Similarities can be seen between the father/daughter relationships in both works. Morbius (played by Walter Pidgeon) is clearly a Prospero, and his daughter Alta (Anne Francis), like Miranda, has never seen men.*

5. *Emergo. William Castle directed the film. Unfortunately, it was difficult to direct the appearance of the skeleton—in every movie theater—where it was scheduled to frighten the audience.*

6. *The Nazis saw too great a similarity between the rocket ships shown in* The Girl in the Moon (*or* By Rocket to the Moon, *as it is sometimes called) and designs for German rocket-weapons. Rocket expert Willie Ley served as a technical consultant on the Lang film.*

7. *Elsa Lanchester again. Mary Shelley's novel, by the way, is subtitled* The Modern Prometheus, *in reference to the Greek god/hero who stole fire from the gods.*

8. The Blob, *directed by Irvin S. Yeaworth. Steve McQueen went on to better things.*

9. The Time Machine *(1960). Based on the H. G. Wells novel, the film was directed by George Pal and features a screenplay by David Duncan.*

10. 2001: A Space Odyssey *(1968). The film helped sell numerous recordings of Strauss waltzes to kids who grew up on rock-and-roll.*

11. *Christopher Lee.*

12. It Came From Outer Space. *The story was based upon a treatment by Ray Bradbury. The film was directed by Jack Arnold, who can be seen playing the part of the newsreel reporter in* Citizen Kane. *This was the first science fiction film shot in 3-D.*

13. *Lugosi, Hungary. (The Hungarian spelling is Lugoj.)*

14. *Ben Chapman.*

15. Rocketship Galileo.

16. *James Arness. He is, of course, much better known for his television roles, such as Matt Dillon in* Gunsmoke.

17. The Day the Earth Stood Still *(1951). The film (directed by Robert Wise) was based on the short story "Farewell to the Master" by Harry Bates.*

18. *Godzilla, Manda, Mothra, and Rodan.*

19. *Lon Chaney, Jr. played the monster.*

Remakes/
Sequels

1. Warren Beatty's film *Heaven Can Wait* is, of course, the most recent remake of the 1941 film classic *Here Comes Mr. Jordan.* In 1947, however, a technicolor sequel to *Here Comes Mr. Jordan* was filmed. The 1947 film tells how a muse named Terpsichore journeys down to earth to play herself in a Broadway musical about the nine muses. What is the name of that film? Who plays Terpsichore?

2. *Bells on Their Toes* is a 1952 sequel to what comedy success?

3. In 1954 *A Farewell to Arms,* the film version of Ernest Hemingway's novel, starred Rock Hudson as Frederic Henry and Jennifer Jones as Catherine Barkley. Who played those roles in the 1932 version?

4. In Fritz Lang's classic film *M,* Peter Lorre plays the child murderer. Who plays the murderer in the 1950 Hollywood remake?

5. The 1952 film *The Clown* stars Red Skelton. With a simple change of profession, *The Clown* is a remake of what 1932 film starring Wallace Beery?

6. Charlton Heston and Stephen Boyd are well known, in part, for their roles in *Ben Hur.* Who play their roles in the 1926 silent film version?

7. The 1946 film *Easy to Wed* is a remake of what 1936 film that starred William Powell, Myrna Loy, Spencer Tracy, and Jean Harlow?

8. *The Jazz Singer* has been made three times. What is the name of Al Jolson's character in the 1927 sound version? Who plays Cantor Rabbinowitz? In the 1953 version, who plays the lead? What is the Jazz Singer's name? Who directed the film? In the 1981 version, who plays the lead? What is the main character's name? Who plays Cantor Rabinovitch?

9. In 1934 Shirley Temple played *Little Miss Marker.* In the 1981 remake, who plays Little Miss Marker? The 1949 film version of the Damon Runyon story is called *Sorrowful Jones.* Who plays Little Miss Marker in the 1949 film? Who plays Sorrowful Jones? Who plays Sorrowful Jones in the 1981 film *Little Miss Marker?*

10. *Silk Stockings* is the 1957 musical remake of what film comedy?

11. The 1959 film *Watusi,* starring George Montgomery, is a sequel to what 1950 film?

12. The 1954 film *Demetrius and the Gladiators,* starring Victor Mature, is a sequel to what film?

13. Here's a quickie: who directed the sequel to *Star Wars—The Empire Strikes Back* (1981)?

14. In the sequel to *Oh God!—Oh God! Book II* (1981)— George Burns returned to play God again. What noted TV personality and author portrays herself in *Oh God! Book II?*

15. The sequel to what film won an Academy Award as Best Picture? (Hint: The film on which the sequel was based also won an Academy Award as Best Picture!)

ANSWERS

1. *The film is* Down to Earth. *Too bad the plot isn't down to earth. Rita Hayworth plays Terpsichore, the muse of dancing and choral song. Roland Culver plays Mr. Jordan.*

2. Bells on Their Toes *is the follow-up to* Cheaper by the Dozen. Cheaper by the Dozen, *starring Clifton Webb and Myrna Loy, tells the story of an efficiency expert and his dozen children. The film was so popular that it grossed nearly $4.5 million dollars.*

3. *In the 1932 film, Gary Cooper plays Frederic Henry and Helen Hayes plays Catherine.*

4. *David Wayne plays the murderer.*

5. The Champ *(1931). The film was again remade (again as a boxing film) with Jon Voight and Ricky Schroeder in 1979.*

6. *Francis X. Bushman and Ramon Navarro.*

7. Easy to Wed *is a remake of* Libeled Lady. *In* Easy to Wed, *Lucille Ball plays the part of Gladys Benton.*

8. *In the 1927 film* The Jazz Singer, *Al Jolson plays Jack Robin (shortened from Jakie Rabbinowitz) and Warner Orland plays Cantor Rabbinowitz. In the 1953 remake, Danny Thomas plays the lead, and the character's name is Jerry Golding. Michael Curtiz directed the 1953 version. In the 1981 film, Neil Diamond plays the lead, and the Jazz Singer's name is Jess Robin. Cantor Rabinovitch is played by Sir Laurence Olivier.*

9. *Sara Stimson plays the Shirley Temple role in the 1981 remake, and Mary Jane Saunders plays the role in the 1949 film. In* Sorrowful Jones, *Bob Hope plays the lead. In 1981,* Sorrowful Jones *was played by Walter Matthau.*

10. Silk Stockings *is the musical version of* Ninotchka *(1939). The musical version was directed by Rouben Mamoulian.*

11. Watusi *is the sequel to* King Solomon's Mines, *starring Stewart Granger and Deborah Kerr.* Watusi *makes use of several scenes from the original film and was made in only fifteen days.*

12. Demetrius and the Gladiators *was the follow-up to* The Robe *(1953).* The Robe *was the first feature film shot in Cinemascope.*

13. *Irvin Kershner directed* The Empire Strikes Back.

14. *Dr. Joyce Brothers appears as herself in* Oh God! Book II. *Not only is Dr. Brothers a noted psychologist, but she also won $64,000 on the TV quiz show* The $64,000 Question *by answering questions about boxing.*

15. *Both* The Godfather *(1972) and* The Godfather, Part II *(1974) won Academy Awards for Best Picture.*

Westerns (and Westerns of Sorts)

1. You have most likely heard of the Cisco Kid, but what film gave us the Waco Kid? In what classic American film can you find the Ringo Kid? The Abilene Kid?

2. In the 1969 film *True Grit,* what popular singer plays the role of La Boeuf?

3. What world-famous singer plays the part of Alias in *Pat Garrett and Billy the Kid*?

4. The 1939 movie serial *The Lone Ranger Rides Again* stars an actor who is much better known for playing another classic western hero. Who is the star? For what role is he better known?

5. What world-famous cowboy star made a guest appearance in Cecil B. De Mille's circus epic *The Greatest Show on Earth*?

6. Marlon Brando has directed only one movie, and it is a western. Can you name it?

7. Only one western movie has received an Oscar for Best Picture. What film? What year? Who stars in the film?

8. Joey cries out, "Come back, Shane." Who plays the part of Joey in *Shane*? Who wrote the novel upon which the film was based?

9. What famous western film shows children torturing a scorpion as part of its opening sequence?

10. What Howard Hawks western was based upon the story "The Blazing Guns on the Chisholm Trail," by Borden Chase?

11. *The Magnificent Seven* (1960) stars Yul Brynner as a gunfighter named Chris. Can you name at least four of the other six movie stars that play Chris's companions?

12. While making a western, star Joel McCrea refused to kill a character that was being played by his young son, and so the script was modified. What was the name of the film?

13. Who played General George Armstrong Custer in the following films?
    Santa Fe Trail (1940)
    They Died With Their Boots On (1941)
    Sitting Bull (1954)
    Little Big Man (1970)

14. If you are a true western fan, you should be able to recite (or figure out) at least one-half of Gene Autry's "Ten Commandments for Cowboys." Can you? (We won't hold you to the exact wording.)

15. Who was the first person to play the Lone Ranger on the screen?

16. The Cincinnati Reds baseball team once autographed a second base bag and sent it to a famous cowboy star. To whom did they send it, and why?

17. In 1941 Republic Pictures issued a film with a most familiar title—*The Great Train Robbery.* Who made the original *Great Train Robbery?* Who stars in the 1941 film?

18. What great Olympic star and football player has a role in the 1928 Tex Ritter movie *Arizona Frontier?*

19. In what silent film can viewers read the following title?

Silk Miller: mingling the oily craftiness of a
Mexican with the deadly treachery of a rattler,
No man's open enemy, and no man's friend.

20. We started this section of western questions with a question about famous Kids, so let's end on that note. In what western can you see Kid Shelleen? Who plays the role?

ANSWERS

1. *The Waco Kid can be seen in Mel Brooks's parody* Blazing Saddles. *The Ringo Kid can be seen in* Stagecoach. *John Wayne plays the part. The Abilene Kid is in John Ford's* Three Godfathers.

2. *Glenn Campbell plays La Boeuf.*

3. *Bob Dylan.* Variety *said of his performance: ". . . his acting is currently limited to an embarrassing assortment of tics, smirks, shrugs, winks, and smiles." Bob Dylan also wrote the title song for the film.*

4. *The star is Duncan Rinaldo. He is much better known for his portrayals of the Cisco Kid.*

5. *William Boyd as Hopalong Cassidy. His oft-quoted advice on how to get along with people was, "Treat children like adults and adults like children."*

6. One-eyed Jacks *(1961). The film turned out to be a box-office failure.*

7. Cimarron *(1931). Richard Dix and Irene Dunne star. Wesley Ruggles, Edward Cronjager, Richard Dix, and Irene Dunne all were nominated for Academy Awards for their work in this film. Glenn Ford and Maria Schell star in the 1961 remake.*

8. *Brandon de Wilde plays the part of Joey. Jack Schaefer wrote the novel.*

9. The Wild Bunch, *a 1969 film directed by Sam Peckinpah. William Holden, Robert Ryan, and Ernest Borgnine are the stars.*

10. Red River. *Both Harry Carey, Sr. and Harry Carey, Jr. appear in this film that stars John Wayne and Montgomery Clift.*

11. *The other six stars are Steve McQueen, Robert Vaughn, Charles Bronson, Horst Buchholz, James Coburn, and Brad Dexter.*

12. Wichita *(1955). In the 1956 film* The First Texan, *Jody McCrea plays Baker and Joel McCrea plays Sam Houston.*

13. *Ronald Reagan in* Santa Fe Trail; *Errol Flynn in* They Died With

Their Boots on; *Douglas Kennedy in* Sitting Bull; *and Richard Mulligan in* Little Big Man.

14. *The Cowboy's Ten Commandments:*
    1. He must not take unfair advantage when facing an enemy.
    2. He must never go back on his word.
    3. He must be gentle with children, elderly people, and animals.
    4. He must not advocate or possess racially or religiously intolerant ideas.
    5. He must help people in distress.
    6. He must be a good worker.
    7. He must keep himself clean in thought, speech, action, and personal habits.
    8. He must respect women, parents, and his nation's laws.
    9. He must not drink or smoke.
    10. The cowboy must be a patriot.

15. *Lee Powell, in the 1938 Republic serial, was the first person to portray the Lone Ranger upon the screen. Chief Thundercloud plays Tonto.*

16. *The Cincinnatti Reds sent the autographed base to Roy Rogers because the boyhood home of the future King of the Cowboys once stood on the current location of second base in Cincinnati's Riverfront Stadium.*

17. *Edwin S. Porter made the original film, which is often called the first American film to tell a story in cinematic terms. Bob Steele stars in the 1941 version.*

18. *Jim Thorpe.*

19. *That title can be seen in* Hell's Hinges, *the 1916 William S. Hart film. The part of Silk Miller is played by Alfred Hollingsworth.*

20. *Kid Shelleen is the run-down cowboy in* Cat Ballou *(1964). The part is played by Lee Marvin. Mr. Marvin received the Academy Award as Best Actor for his role.*

Sports Films

1. Can you name three films in which Babe Ruth appears?

2. Here is a question for Boston Red Sox fans. We all know that Anthony Perkins plays Jimmy Piersall in *Fear Strikes Out* (1957). What Hall of Famer is played by Bart Burns in that film?

3. *It's Good to Be Alive* (1975) is the film biography of Roy Campanella. Who plays Campanella?

4. In 1926 football star Red Grange made his film debut. What is the name of the film?

5. What actor made his screen debut as a boxer in the 1940 film *Golden Gloves*—and did his own boxing in the film?

6. In *The Winning Team,* Ronald Reagan plays what Hall of Fame pitcher?

7. Sports greats Babe Didrikson Zaharias, Betty Hicks, Gussie Moran, and Alice Marble can all be seen in what 1952 sports-centered Spencer Tracy/Katharine Hepburn film?

8. What is the name of the film directed by Robert Aldrich that features a football game played between convicts and prison guards?

9. Identify the great racehorse that was the subject of a 1949 screen biography starring Shirley Temple, Lon McCallister, and Barry Fitzgerald. (Hint: The horse's sire was Hard Tack and its dam was Swing Out. In 1938 this horse was voted Horse of the Year.)

10. In what bullfighting film did cameraman James Wong

Howe have bullfighters fight the bulls with cameras strapped to the men's waists in order to get close-ups of the bull passing under the cape?

11. The 1951 film *Follow the Sun* (directed by Sidney Lanfield) is the story of what professional golfer? Who plays the golfer?

12. Another 1951 film concerns the adventures of a cat that inherits a baseball team. What is the name of the cat (the cat's name is the title of the film)?

13. *Hard, Fast and Beautiful* (1951), a film about a woman playing professional tennis, was directed by what woman?

14. One of the great boxing movies of all time is the 1949 movie *The Set-up*. It was based upon a poem by Joseph Moncure March. Who directed the film, and who plays the lead—the part of a boxer who refuses to throw a fight?

15. *The Other Side of the Mountain* (1975) and *The Other Side of the Mountain, Part II* (1977) are films about a skiing champion who is crippled in an accident and who goes on to become a teacher. The film was based upon the life of what skier? Who plays the skier in both parts?

ANSWERS

1. *Babe Ruth can be seen in three movies:* Heading Home *(1920),* The Ninth Inning *(1942), and* The Pride of the Yankees *(1942). The latter film is a biopic of Lou Gehrig. Gary Cooper plays Lou in that film.*

2. *If you said Ted Williams, you are wrong. Bart Burns plays the part of Joe Cronin.*

3. *Paul Winfield plays the part of "Campy."*

4. *Red Grange made his screen debut in* One Minute to Play. *Music for the film includes the tune, "Red Grange Collegiate Gambol," played by the Red Grange Quartet.*

5. *Robert Ryan. He has only one line in the entire film. In his screen debut he says: "I thought you could get me more."*

6. *Ronald Reagan plays Grover Cleveland Alexander in this 1952 film.*

7. Pat and Mike *shows Katharine Hepburn (a good athlete in her own right) playing tennis and golf with those superstars.*

8. The Longest Yard *(1974), starring Burt Reynolds.*

9. *Seabiscuit* (The Story of Seabiscuit). *Ads for the film stated, "It's the true story of a gallant stallion whose fight for fame brought an old-timer his big dream and two young-timers their big love."*

10. The Brave Bulls *(1951), directed and produced by Robert Rossen.*

11. Follow the Sun *is the story of Ben Hogan. Glenn Ford plays the lead. The film also stars Anne Baxter and Dennis O'Keefe.*

12. Rhubarb *is the cat that owned a ball team. The film was based upon the hilarious novel by H. Allen Smith.*

13. Hard, Fast and Beautiful, *based upon a John R. Tunis novel, was directed by Ida Lupino.*

14. The Set-up *was directed by Robert Wise and stars Robert Ryan.*

15. *The skier in real life was Jill Kinmont. She is played by Marilyn Hassett in the movies.*

Films from Comic Strips

1. Joe Palooka, the famous boxer in comic strips, was brought to the screen in 1934 and again in 1944. Who plays Joe Palooka in each version? (A different actor each time.)

2. In the film versions of *Blondie,* the great comic strip created by Chic Young, who plays Blondie? Who plays Dagwood? Who plays Mr. Dithers?

3. Bud Duncan plays this comic-strip hillbilly on the screen. The character was created by Billy DeBeck. What's the name of the hillbilly?

4. Who is Bingo?

5. When Roger Vadim brought the comic-book heroine Barbarella to the screen, who played Barbarella?

6. What comic-strip character was created by Peter O'Donnell and Jim Holdaway and was portrayed on the screen in 1966 by Monica Vitti?

7. In the film *Up Front,* David Wayne plays Joe. Tom Ewell plays Willie. These famous World War II characters were created by what cartoonist?

8. In the 1954 film based on the Harold Foster comic strip character Prince Valiant, who plays Prince Valiant?

9. In 1927 Marion Davies played what noted comic-strip character, a character that helped to popularize the plight of the working girl in America?

10. The 1982 film *Annie* is not the first film based upon the Harold Gray comic strip. Who plays Annie in the 1932 film *Little Orphan Annie*?

11. Al Capp's Lil Abner was first brought to the screen in 1940. Who played Lil Abner then? Who plays the famous hillbilly in the 1959 screen musical?

12. In 1957, Jerry Lewis brought to the screen what famous George Baker comic-strip/comic-book character?

13. Who plays Emperor Ming the Merciless in the Flash Gordon serials (*Flash Gordon*, 1936; *Flash Gordon's Trip to Mars*, 1938; *Flash Gordon Conquers the Universe*, 1940)?

14. When Jungle Jim was brought to the screen, who played Jungle Jim?

15. What comic-strip character does Kirk Alyn play in the movies?

ANSWERS

1. *Joe Palooka was played by Stuart Irwin in 1934 and by Joe Kirkwood a decade later. Ham Fisher created the comic strip character.*

2. *Penny Singleton plays Blondie, Arthur Lake plays Dagwood, and Jonathan Hale plays Mr. Dithers.*

3. *Snuffy Smith.*

4. *Bingo is the name of the dog that plays Sandy in the 1982 musical film* Annie.

5. *Barbarella is played by Jane Fonda, who was Roger Vadim's wife at the time. Terry Southern wrote the script for this 1967 movie, and the great pantomimist Marcel Marceau has a small role.*

6. *Monica Vitti plays Modesty Blaise in the film of that name directed by Joseph Losey.*

7. *Bill Maudlin created the GI characters Joe and Willie.*

8. *Robert Wagner plays Prince Valiant. Heavyweight prizefighter Primo Carnera also has a role in that movie.*

9. *Marion Davies plays Tillie the Toiler from the comic strip of the same name. The comic strip by Russell Channing Westover made its first appearance in the New York American on January 14, 1921.*

10. *Mitzi Green was the first actress to play Little Orphan Annie. In the comic strip, of course, Annie's eyes (until 1947) were without pupils.*

11. *Granville Owen played Lil Abner in 1940; Peter Parrish plays Lil Abner in the 1959 film of the hit musical comedy.*

12. *Jerry Lewis plays Sad Sack in a movie directed by George Marshall. Peter Lorre also appears in the film.*

13. *Charles Middleton plays Ming. He can also be seen in such other films as* The Grapes of Wrath *(1940) and* The Black Arrow *(1949). He died in 1949. Buster Crabbe, of course, plays Flash Gordon.*

14. *Johnny Weismuller, who is better known for his Tarzan role.*

15. *Kirk Alyn plays Superman in the 1948 serial and in the 1950 serial,* Atomic Man Vs. Superman. *Christopher Reeve, of course, plays the man of steel in the 1978 film, directed by Richard Donner, and in the 1981 sequel. The Superman character was created by Joe Siegel and Joe Schuster, who sold all the rights to their creation for a paltry $130.00.*

Musicals

1. "Something's Gotta Give," "Dream History of the Beat," "Sluefoot," "Welcome Egg Head," and "C-A-T Spells Cat" are a few of the musical numbers from what Fred Astaire film? What orchestra played the music for the sound track?

2. What was the first musical shot in two-color technicolor?

3. Fred Astaire dances on walls and ceilings, and performs "I Left My Hat in Haiti" in what 1951 musical?

4. A sign tells us that Roger Bond and his Yankee Clippers are appearing at the Hibiscus Hotel in Miami, Florida. So what's the musical we are watching?

5. The Fan-Dango ballroom is just one set, and "The Rich Man's Frug" is just one of the numbers, in what musical film?

6. Although the Broadway score for *Paint Your Wagon* features songs by Alan Jay Lerner and Frederick Loewe, what well-known composer/conductor added new songs to the 1969 film version?

7. "Who are You?" and "The Greeks Have a Word For It" are two songs from the film of what Rodgers and Hart musical? Who play the male leads in the film?

8. Nancy Carroll steps out of a giant shoe and dances to the tune of "Dancing to Save Your Sole" in what 1930 film?

9. When Judy Garland sings "You Made Me Love You" in the film *Broadway Melody of 1935,* she sings the song to a photograph of what movie star?

10. When Deborah Kerr sang in *The King and I,* whose voice was dubbed for her songs?

11. José Ferrer plays what composer in the 1954 MGM film *Deep in My Heart?*

12. In the 1946 film *Till The Clouds Roll By* (the story of Jerome Kern), who plays the role of singer Marilyn Miller?

ANSWERS

1. *These numbers are from* Daddy Long Legs. *Leslie Caron is Fred Astaire's dancing partner in this film. The music is played by Ray Anthony and his orchestra.*

2. *The 1929 film* On With the Show *was the first musical to be filmed in the two-color technicolor process. The film stars Joe E. Brown and Betty Compson.*

3. Royal Wedding. *The screenplay, by the way, was written by Alan Jay Lerner.*

4. Flying Down to Rio *(1933). A song from this film, "The Carioca," was nominated for an Academy Award. The film was based upon a play written by Anne Caldwell.*

5. Sweet Charity *(1969). The musical was based upon a Fellini film,* The Nights of Cabiria.

6. *André Previn.*

7. The Boys From Syracuse *(1940). Based on Shakespeare's Comedy of Errors, the musical features Joe Penner and Allan Jones.*

8. *The film is* Paramount on Parade, *a film that presents thirty-five of Paramount's top performers, including Richard Arlen, Gary Cooper, William Powell, and Jack Oakie.*

9. *She sings to a photograph of Clark Gable.*

10. *Marni Nixon did the behind-the-scenes singing.*

11. *José Ferrer portrays the composer Sigmund Romberg. That film was the last all-star musical biography produced at MGM.*

12. *Judy Garland plays Marilyn Miller and sings two songs in that film: "Who" and "Look for the Silver Lining."*

Cartoons

1. What cartoon character has Aloysius as a middle name?

2. What cartoon character was based upon the Lana Turner character Bunny Smith from *Week-end at the Waldorf* (1945)?

3. What was the first Bugs Bunny cartoon?

4. What was Mickey Mouse's original name?

5. For what world-famous cartoon and comic-strip character did Jack Mercer and Floyd Buckley supply the voice?

6. In 1970 cartoonist Robert Crumb introduced the first full-length X-rated animated film. What was the name of his X-rated character?

7. What cartoon character says, "Thuffering Thucotash"?

8. Helen Kane's face inspired what well-known cartoon character?

9. What cartoon character was created by Pat Sullivan?

10. The Blue Meanies launch a missile attack in what well-known animated film?

11. Jim Backus supplied the voice for what cartoon character?

12. What is the name of the cartoon character (featured in UPA cartoons) who is a little boy who speaks only in sounds?

13. A Mickey Mouse cartoon plays an important role in what Preston Sturges film?

14. Fred Quimby is associated with what very popular cartoon team?

15. What cartoon character has a niece named Knothead and a nephew called Splinter?

16. What cartoon characters dance with Gene Kelly in the film *Anchors Aweigh*?

ANSWERS

1. *Aloysius is one of Daffy Duck's middle names. Daffy was created by Bob Clampett; Mel Blanc supplied Daffy's voice.*

2. *Toodles, a sexy cat created by William Hanna and Joseph Barbera, appeared in the MGM cartoon* Springtime for Thomas *(1945). Toodles was based upon Lana Turner's role.*

3. *Bugs Bunny (with Mel Blanc supplying the voice) made his film debut in the 1940 cartoon* A Wild Hare. *(Is that rabbit really a hare?) Elmer Fudd also made his debut in that film. Mel Blanc also supplied the voice for Elmer Fudd.*

4. *Mickey Mouse was originally called Mortimer Mouse. Mickey was drawn by Ub Iwerks of the Walt Disney staff.*

5. *Jack Mercer and Floyd Buckley supplied the voice for Popeye. A number of other people also supplied Popeye's voice over the years. An actress, Mae Questel, did Popeye's voice for six or seven cartoons.*

6. Fritz the Cat *(1970). A sequel (also X-rated) was released four years later—*The Nine Lives of Fritz the Cat.

7. *Sylvester, with voice supplied by (who else?) Mel Blanc.*

8. *Betty Boop. Helen Kane also supplied the voice for Betty in the Betty Boop cartoons.*

9. *Felix the Cat. Felix (who was named by Paramount producer John King) was drawn by Pat Sullivan's assistant, Otto Mesmer.*

10. Yellow Submarine, *based upon the Beatles' Sergeant Pepper's Lonely Hearts Club Band.*

11. *Jim Backus provided the voice for the near-sighted Mister Magoo.*

12. *Gerald McBoing Boing (created by Stephen Bosustow) speaks only in "boings."*

13. Sullivan's Travels *(1941). A film director played by Joel McCrea is deeply moved when he watches prisoners in a chain gang laugh uproariously over the antics of Goofy.*

14. *Fred Quimby (1886–1960) was the head of MGM's short-subject department for many years. If you saw any Tom and Jerry cartoons, you would have seen his name featured prominently in the credits, for he was executive producer on those films. Tom and Jerry were drawn by William Hanna and Joseph Barbera.*

15. *Woody Woodpecker.*

16. *Tom and Jerry dance with Gene Kelly in* Anchors Aweigh *(1945). They also swim with Esther Williams in the film* Dangerous When Wet *(1953).*

FREEZE FRAME

General Quiz #3

1. What silent film star is associated with Falcon's Lair?

2. In 1947, newspaper headlines and stories seethed with news about the "Hollywood Ten": those actors, writers, producers, and directors who refused to cooperate with the notorious House of Un-American Activities Committee. Name any four members of the "Hollywood Ten."

3. *The Gay Illiterate,* published in 1944, is the autobiography of what Hollywood gossip columnist?

4. Liberace plays a casket salesman in what film?

5. In what 1965 French film do all the characters sing?

6. Can you identify Matthew "Stymie" Beard?

7. What actress (who appears in such films as *The Mask of Dimitros, Destination Tokyo,* and *Hotel Berlin*) was once married to a son of Franklin Delano Roosevelt?

8. Bonaventure was the middle name of what all-time great screen star?

9. What does the G. stand for in Edward G. Robinson?

10. We'll give you the name of the horses; can you tell us what cowboy stars rode them?
    a. Tarzan
    b. Topper
    c. Fritz
    d. Tony
    e. White Flash

11. During the early 1940s, telephones were often humorously referred to as "Ameches." Why?

12. Although film fans tend to think of Fred Astaire as always dancing with Ginger Rogers, he does dance with other women in his films. Who is his dancing partner in *Easter Parade* (1948)? Who is his dancing partner in *Silk Stockings* (1957)?

13. What does the "M" stand for in *Dial M for Murder?*

14. What American film comedian, his career ruined by scandal, directed a few films under the name William Goodrich?

15. What was MGM's famous motto?

16. In *Public Enemy* (1939), what actress gets a grapefruit pushed into her face by James Cagney?

17. According to Milton Caniff, creator of the comic strip "Terry and the Pirates," the famed Dragon Lady in his strip was inspired by a noted movie actress. Can you name the actress?

18. In 1974, what famous motion-picture actress was appointed United States ambassador to Ghana?

19. What cowboy star gave up his screen career to become lieutenant governor of Nevada?

20. In the *Lone Ranger* series, Tonto is an Indian. In the film *Harry and Tonto,* who or what is Tonto?

21. In *Viva Zapata* (1952), Alan Reed plays Pancho Villa. In 1934, Wallace Beery played Pancho Villa in *Viva Villa.* Who plays the role of Pancho Villa in *Villa Rides!* (1968)?

22. In the 1953 animated film *Peter Pan,* what well-known child star supplied the voice for Peter Pan?

ANSWERS

1. *Falcon's Lair was the name of Rudolph Valentino's home. The house was built for his second wife—Natacha Rambova—but she never lived there.*

2. *The "Hollywood Ten" consisted of: Alvah Bessie, Herbert Biberman, Lester Cole, Edward Dmytryk, Ring Lardner, Jr., John Howard Lawson, Albert Martz, Sam Ornitz, Adrian Scot, and Dalton Trumbell.*

3. *Louella Parsons wrote* The Gay Illiterate.

4. *Liberace plays a casket salesman in the 1965 film* The Loved One *(based upon Evelyn Waugh's novel).*

5. *All the characters sing all their lines in* The Umbrellas of Cherbourg, *written and directed by Jacques Demy. The music was composed by Michel Lombard.*

6. *Matthew "Stymie" Beard is the bald-headed black boy who wears the derby in* Our Gang *comedies. He also played Cleon on the TV sitcom* Sanford and Son.

7. *Fay Emerson. Elliott Roosevelt was the second of her three husbands.*

8. *On April 5, 1900, Spencer Bonaventure Tracy was born in Milwaukee, Wisconsin.*

9. *Goldenberg. His real name was Emanuel Goldenberg. He once told a reporter, "I kept the initials E. G., but I don't know to this day why I chose Robinson as a last name. If I had to do it again, I'd take a shorter name. You have no idea how long it takes to write Edward G. Robinson for a flock of autograph hunters."*

10.   *a. Tarzan was Ken Maynard's horse*
    b. Topper was ridden by Hopalong Cassidy
    c. Fritz belonged to William S. Hart
    d. Tony was ridden by Tom Mix
    e. Tex Ritter rode White Flash

11. *Telephones were known as "Ameches" because Don Ameche*

played the inventor of the telephone in The Story of Alexander Graham Bell *(1939).*

12. *Judy Garland danced with Fred Astaire in* Easter Parade. *Cyd Charisse was his partner in* Silk Stockings.

13. *In London, there is a telephone exchange called Maida Vale. The letter M is the first letter of that exchange.*

14. *Roscoe "Fatty" Arbuckle. His first directorial assignment was a Marion Davis picture for William Randolph Hearst's film company. Ironically, Hearst's newspapers had been the most insistent about the comedian's guilt in the death of Virginia Rappe at one of Fatty's so-called "Wild Parties."*

15. *MGM's motto was* Ars Gratia Artis—Art for Art's Sake. *Tell that one to the stockholders.*

16. *Mae Clark.*

17. *Joan Crawford inspired the Dragon Lady.*

18. *Shirley Temple Black.*

19. *Rex Bell. His given name was George Bedlam.*

20. *Tonto is a cat. Art Carney received an Academy Award for his role in the film. The cat did not.*

21. *Yul Brynner plays Pancho Villa in that film. The script was written by Robert Towne and Sam Peckinpah, but* Villa Rides! *was directed by Buzz Kulik.*

22. *Bobby Driscoll (1937–1968). He also appears in Walt Disney's* Treasure Island. *He received an Academy Award for Best Child Actor in 1949.*

BEHIND THE
SILVER SCREEN

Directors/ Producers

1. What film producer told the *New York Times,* "I can only hope that on my tombstone are the words: '*Annie,* she is the one I was working for' "?

2. In 1932 Benn Levy directed a film called *Lord Camber's Ladies.* The producer of that film, however, went on to win worldwide fame as a director himself—a director who is much better known than Benn Levy. Who was that producer?

3. Why did producer David O. Selznick have to pay a $5,000 fine to the Motion Picture Producers Association in 1939?

4. H. B. Warner and Cecil B. De Mille can be seen on the screen in what classic film?

5. The first major film to be produced in Hollywood, California was directed by Cecil B. De Mille in 1913. Can you name the film?

6. What two men—who would eventually go on to become noted film directors themselves—worked as film editors on Orson Welles's *Citizen Kane?*

7. What director said of Walt Disney, "Disney, of course, has the best casting. If he doesn't like an actor, he just tears him up"?

8. William Cameron Menzies—the art designer for *Gone With the Wind*—directed what 1950s science fiction film?

9. Singer Judy Collins produced and co-directed a documentary film about what noted conductor and teacher?

10. Singer Bob Dylan produced and directed what 3-hour-and-55-minute film?

11. The director originally wanted to call his film *Sleep No More*. Science fiction fans know it by another title. The main character is named Dr. Miles Bennell. Name the film and its director.

12. Sidney Poitier directed what 1974 and 1975 films with Bill Cosby as his co-star?

13. Who directed the last major silent film made in Hollywood? What was the film's title?

14. What well-known movie actor directed the 1955 film *A Man Alone*?

15. What film is the only feature film directed by cinematographer James Wong Howe? (Hint: the movie features the Harlem Globetrotters.)

16. Name one film directed by the noted actor Walter Matthau.

17. When Josef Von Sternberg walked out on *The Masked Bride* (1925), what director took over and finished the picture?

18. This director once wrote an unproduced play about a pool hall and its characters. The title of the play was *Corner Pocket*. He is, however, far better known for a film on the same subject. Can you identify the director?

19. What person is often credited with producing the first million-dollar picture? (He is also given credit for calling certain top motion picture actors and actresses "stars").

20. Name the noted film director who started his career as an actor and who played the part of John Wilkes Booth in *The Birth of a Nation*?

21. In 1971, Jack Lemmon directed his first movie. What is the one and only film directed by Jack Lemmon?

22. What film did Howard Hawks co-direct with Howard Hughes?

23. In what film produced by Stanley Kramer is the speech of a New York taxicab driver so unintelligible that subtitles are used to translate "New Yorkese" to English?

24. What is John Ford's only Civil War film (not counting a segment from *How the West Was Won*)?

25. Walt Disney brought two children's stories by Felix Salten to the screen. What were they?

26. Who was the Canadian-born film director who directed such films as *Heidi* (1937), *Rebecca of Sunnybrook Farm* (1938), and *Sands of Iwo Jima* (1949)?

27. Alfred Hitchcock was nominated for an Academy Award as Best Director five times, but he never won (although one of his pictures, *Rebecca,* did win an Oscar for Best Picture). Can you name the five films for which Hitchcock received Academy Award nominations as Best Director?

28. The film star who plays Chopin in the 1945 film *A Song to Remember* (1945) went on to direct such films as *The Naked Prey* (1966) and *Beach Red* (1967). Who is he?

29. In 1965 Bosley Crowther wrote: "If the threat of Frank Sinatra as a film director is judged by his first try . . . it is clear that there need be no apprehension among the directors of the Screen Directors Guild." What film was directed and produced by Frank Sinatra?

30. John Huston said of one of his films, "Originally I wanted to do the movie with two friends—Clark Gable and Humphrey Bogart. However, every time I started to think about the film, another project came up and finally I just about gave up hope. Then suddenly in 1974, producer

John Foreman interested Allied Artists and Columbia Pictures in jointly financing the movie. I think it's one of the greatest adventure stories ever written." What film is Mr. Huston talking about? What stars ended up playing the roles originally conceived for Gable and Bogart?

31. Writing for the March 7, 1914 issue of *The Moving Picture World,* Louis Harrison called D. W. Griffith's first feature-length production "a fascinating work of high artistry." What film was Mr. Harrison referring to?

32. What future film director can be seen as the owner of a racing car in the "modern" section of D. W. Griffith's *Intolerance* (1916)?

33. Because his parents were strict Calvinists, this writer/director didn't see his first movie until he was seventeen years old. The first movie that he saw was Walt Disney's *Living Desert,* but he went on to write *Taxi Driver, Blue Collar,* and *Rolling Thunder.* He directed *Blue Collar* (1979) and *American Gigolo* (1980). Who is he?

34. The 1914 film of *The Merchant of Venice* was the first feature film directed by a woman. Who directed it?

35. Who was the first film director to earn a million dollars for directing a single picture? What is the picture?

36. Who was the first woman to be named president of production of a major United States film company?

37. A 1967 James Bond film features six directors. Can you name any two of the six directors of *Casino Royale?*

38. *Manhattan Carnival* was the first talking film to be directed by a woman. Who was she?

39. The film is titled *Andy Warhol's Frankenstein,* but it was neither directed nor written by Andy Warhol. Who wrote and directed that 1974 film?

ANSWERS

1. *The man who said that was Ray Stark, the producer of* Annie *(1982). The film was directed by John Huston.*

2. *Alfred Hitchcock produced (but did not direct)* Lord Camber's Ladies.

3. *David O. Selznick was ordered to pay a $5,000 fine to the Motion Picture Producers Association because he dared to use profanity—the word "damn"—in his epic film* Gone With the Wind.

4. Sunset Boulevard *(1950). Another great film director/producer, Erich Von Stroheim, can also be seen in this film. He plays the butler Max von Meyerling.*

5. The Squaw Man *was the first major film to be made in Hollywood, California.*

6. *Robert Wise and Mark Robson. Films directed by Robson include:* The Bridges at Toko Ri *(1955),* Peyton Place *(1957), and* Von Ryan's Express *(1965). Robert Wise directed such films as* The Set-up *(1949),* Run Silent, Run Deep *(1958), and* The Sound of Music *(1965).*

7. *Alfred Hitchcock. He was quite fond of saying bad things about actors himself.*

8. Invaders From Mars *(1953). William Cameron Menzies also designed and directed an earlier sci-fi film,* Things to Come, *based upon the book by H. G. Wells.*

9. *Antonia Brico. The film shows how difficult it is for a woman conductor to practice her profession.*

10. Renaldo and Clara *(1977). The film was not very well received by audiences and critics.*

11. The Invasion of the Body Snatchers *(1956). The director was Don Siegel.*

12. *Sidney Poitier directed* Uptown Saturday Night *in 1974. The film was so successful that the 1975 sequel was titled (appropriately enough)* Let's Do It Again.

13. *The last major silent film was directed by Mel Brooks. The film was* Silent Movie *(1976). Before the Mel Brooks film, the last major silent film was Charlie Chaplin's* Modern Times.

14. *Ray Milland directed* A Man Alone *(1955).*

15. Go, Man, Go *(1954). In that film Sidney Poitier played Inman Jackson, one of the original Globetrotters.*

16. *Walter Matthau directed* Gangster Story *in 1961.*

17. *When Von Sternberg left, Christy Cabanne took over.*

18. *Robert Rossen. His pool-hall film is* The Hustler *(1961), starring Paul Newman and Jackie Gleason.*

19. *Carl Laemmle (affectionately called "Uncle Carl"), according to some sources (see his obituary in* Time *magazine, for example), produced the first million-dollar movie. It was the 1922 film* Foolish Wives, *directed by Erich Von Stroheim.*

20. *Raoul Walsh. It was the second time that Walsh had appeared in the same story. Walsh's first acting job was in San Antonio, Texas, where he was an extra who rode a horse on a treadmill in* The Clansman, *a play based upon the novel by Thomas Dixon, Jr. That same novel inspired* Birth of a Nation. *During the making of* Birth of a Nation, *Raoul Walsh injured his leg (just as John Wilkes Booth had done) while making the leap from Lincoln's box to the stage.*

21. Kotch, *which stars Walter Matthau, was directed by Jack Lemmon.*

22. *Howard Hawks and Howard Hughes co-directed Jane Russell in* The Outlaw *(1946).*

23. *The subtitle gag was used in* So This Is New York *(1941), starring radio performer Henry Morgan. The film was based on Ring Lardner's* The Big Town.

24. *John Ford's only Civil War film is* The Horse Soldiers *(1959). Hoot Gibson has the part of Brown in this film, which stars John Wayne and William Holden.*

25. Bambi *and* Perri *are the two Felix Salten books that were brought to the screen by Walt Disney.*

26. *Those films, and many, many others, were directed by Allan*

Dwan, who was born Joseph Aloysius Dwan in Toronto, Canada in 1895.

27. *Alfred Hitchcock was nominated for his work on* Rebecca *(1940),* Life Boat *(1944),* Spellbound *(1940),* Rear Window *(1954), and* Psycho *(1960).*

28. *Cornel Wilde directed those films. The* Naked Prey, *filmed in Africa, contains only a few spoken words and is entirely without dialogue.*

29. *Frank Sinatra produced and directed* None But the Brave *(1965). He also stars in it. Another famous singer, Tommy Sands, plays Lieutenant Blair in the movie.*

30. *Sean Connery and Michael Caine play the lead roles in* The Man Who Would Be King.

31. *D. W. Griffith's first feature-length production (four reels) was* Judith of Bethulia, *starring Blanche Sweet.*

32. *Tod Browning (1882–1962).* Freaks *is his most notorious film, but he directed over forty other films, including the 1931* Dracula.

33. *Paul Schrader. He also wrote the film script for* Raging Bull *(1981).*

34. *Louis Weber. She also directed other movies, including a 1916 film about birth control,* Where Are My Children?

35. *Mike Nichols earned a million dollars for directing* The Graduate *(1967).*

36. *On January 2, 1980, Ms. Sherry Lansing was named president of production at Twentieth Century Fox.*

37. *The seven directors of* Casino Royale *were: John Huston, Ken Hughes, Val Guest, Robert Parrish, Joe McGrath, and Richard Talmadge.*

38. Manhattan Carnival *(1928) was directed by Dorothy Arzner*

39. *Paul Morrissey wrote and directed Andy Warhol's horror film. The film was made in 3-D.*

Writers

1. Mrs. Aurania Ellerbeck Rouverol's second play, *Skidding,* opened on Broadway on May 21, 1928. The play eventually inspired what famous series of sixteen films?

2. What American writer of detective fiction wrote the screenplays for *Algiers* (1938), *Stand Up and Fight* (1939), and *Gypsy Wildcat* (1944)?

3. Margaret Laurence wrote a novel called *A Jest of God.* The book was used as the basis for what Joanne Woodward film? Who directed it? (Hint: It was the first film he directed.)

4. Can you name the screenwriter who wrote the screenplays to *One Flew Over the Cuckoo's Nest, Melvin and Howard,* and *Shoot the Moon?*

5. What actress wrote the novels *The Incredible Charlie Carewe* and *A Place Called Saturday?* (Lucille Langhanke was her given name.)

6. What noted silent film director (*The Four Horsemen of the Apocalypse, The Prisoner of Zenda, Scaramouche,* etc.) wrote the 1939 novel about a bullfighter named Chuchito—*Mars in the House of Death?*

7. F. Scott Fitzgerald was the co-author of a screenplay (with Edward E. Paramore) that was based upon a novel by Erich Maria Remarque. Can you identify the 1938 film?

8. What noted literary critic wrote (and directed) *Duet for Cannibals* (1969)?

9. When Shelley Winters wrote her autobiography, she quoted the following lines on her dedication page:
   Have ye leisure, comfort, calm,
   Shelter, food, love's gentle balm?
   Or what is it ye buy so dear
   With your pain and with your fear?
   What poet is she quoting?

10. What well-known comedian wrote a children's book called *Gertrude and Heathcliffe,* the story of two seagulls?

11. When Elizabeth Taylor was a teenager, studio publicists credited the actress with writing a book called *Nibbles and Me.* Who was Nibbles?

12. The novelist Elinor Glyn plays herself in what 1927 classic?

13. Walt Disney's *Bongo* (part of the longer film *Fun and Fancy Free*) is based upon a story by what Nobel Prize winner in literature?

14. For what Stanley Kramer film did noted children's book writer Dr. Seuss provide the story? (Along with Allan Scott, Dr. Seuss also co-authored the screenplay.)

15. Griffith's 1918 film *Hearts of the World* features a scenario written by M. Gaston de Tolignac, translated into English by Captain Victor Mauer. Both names, however, are pseudonyms of a much better-known cinematic artist. Who really wrote the scenario and then pretended to have translated it?

ANSWERS

1. Skidding *introduced the famous Hardy family to the American public and provided the backbone for the Andy Hardy films.*

2. *James M. Cain, author of* The Postman Always Rings Twice *and many other books, wrote those screenplays.*

3. *The film based upon* A Jest of God *is* Rachel, Rachel *(1968), the first film directed by Paul Newman.*

4. *Bo Goldman wrote those film scripts.*

5. *Mary Astor wrote those novels. She also wrote two highly successful autobiographies,* My Story *and* A Life on Film.

6. *Rex Ingram (Reginald Hitchcock) wrote the novel.*

7. Three Comrades.

8. *Susan Sontag wrote* Duet for Cannibals. *Writing for* Vogue *magazine, Frederic Tuten called the film "a witty, bone-dry serio-comedy that fascinates and disturbs in turn. . . ."*

9. *What poet would Shelley quote but Shelley?*

10. *Red Skelton. In his comedy monologues he would often tell Gertrude-and-Heathcliffe jokes and would, by folding his hands into his armpits, impersonate the two birds flying.*

11. *Nibbles was Elizabeth Taylor's pet chipmunk. A copy of the book would be a collector's item.*

12. *Elinor Glyn plays herself in* IT, *starring Clara Bow. It was this film that gave Ms. Bow the nickname "the IT girl."*

13. *Sinclair Lewis (1885–1951) wrote the story of Bongo. Many of his novels, of course—Arrowsmith, Babbitt, and Elmer Gantry, for instance—have been brought to the screen.*

14. *Dr. Seuss provided the story for* The 5,000 Fingers of Dr. T *(1953). The film stars Peter Lind Hayes, Mary Healy, and Tommy Retig.*

15. *Both names were pseudonyms used by Griffith himself. He used* *these pseudonyms more than once. Captain Victor Mauer, for example, is given scenario credit for A* Romance of Happy Valley *(1919). For* Dream Street *(1921), D. W. Griffith wrote under the name Roy Sinclair.*

The Casting Office

1. Although Ingrid Bergman gave a fine performance as Maria in *For Whom the Bell Tolls,* she was not the original choice for the role. Another actress had been cast for the part and, in fact, had been on location with the film for three weeks before Ms. Bergman replaced her. Who was the original Maria?

2. After a screen test, a talent scout filed the following report about the actor: "Can't act. Can't sing. Slightly bald. Can dance a little." What actor did not measure up to the talent scout's expectations?

3. Although Gloria Swanson turned in a great performance as Norma Desmond in *Sunset Boulevard* (1950), Ms. Swanson was not the first actress to whom that role was offered. Who turned down the part?

4. Who was first offered the role of Bonnie in *Bonnie and Clyde?*

5. In 1938, what baseball star was offered the opportunity to play Tarzan in the movies, but turned it down?

6. What Hollywood actress was seriously considered for the role of Scarlett O'Hara in *Gone With the Wind,* but lost out because she was "living in sin" with Charlie Chaplin?

7. Who replaced Marilyn Monroe in the movie *How to Be Very Very Popular?*

8. When Richard Zanuck was head of Twentieth Century

Fox, he offered the role of the Sundance Kid from *Butch Cassidy and The Sundance Kid* to Paul Newman. To whom did he offer the part of Butch Cassidy?

9. In the 1933 live-action film version of *Alice in Wonderland,* a number of Hollywood superstars were assigned parts. What characters from *Alice in Wonderland* did the following persons play?
   Gary Cooper
   W. C. Fields
   Cary Grant
   Richard Arlen

10. Who was originally cast to play the lead (Indiana Jones) in *Raiders of the Lost Ark* before Harrison Ford took over?

11. Who was originally offered the role of Lawrence in David Lean's *Lawrence of Arabia* (1962)?

ANSWERS

1. *The first Maria was Vera Zorina. When she was replaced, she sued Paramount Pictures for breach of contract, and Paramount settled with her. It took a while for Ms. Zorina's hair to grow back.*

2. *Fred Astaire was the actor who did not do so well on his screen test. As it turned out, he could dance a little.*

3. *Mae West was originally offered the role of Norma Desmond.*

4. *Tuesday Weld was offered the role that finally went to Faye Dunaway.*

5. *Lou Gehrig was offered the role, but he turned it down.*

6. *Paulette Goddard.*

7. *Sheree North.*

8. *The role of Butch Cassidy was offered to Steve McQueen. Steve McQueen turned it down over a conflict about who would get top billing. Paul Newman took the part of Butch Cassidy, and Robert Redford, of course, became the Sundance Kid.*

9. *Gary Cooper plays the White Knight; W. C. Fields plays Humpty Dumpty; Cary Grant plays the Mock Turtle; and Richard Arlen plays the Cheshire Cat.*

10. *Tom Selleck was offered the role, but he had to pass it up because of his commitment to his television series.*

11. *Albert Finney. He turned down the part because it would have required him to sign a five-year Hollywood contract.*

Behind the Scenes

1. What do Walt Disney, Jim Macdonald, and Wayne Allwine all have in common?

2. Who dubbed the songs for Eddie Bracken in the 1945 film *Out of This World*?

3. In the 1959 film *Porgy and Bess*, Sidney Poitier plays Porgy. But who provided the singing voice for Porgy? Who plays Bess? Who provided the singing voice for Bess?

4. Only once did Harold Lloyd use a stunt double in a film. Name the film and the reason.

5. Who dubbed the singing voice for Stan Laurel in the film *Way Out West*?

6. In the Donald O'Connor and Francis the Talking Mule films, what actor supplied Francis's voice?

7. When Edmund Purdom appeared in the film version of *The Student Prince,* who did the singing for Mr. Purdom on the sound track?

8. In reviewing a certain film, the Legion of Decency suggested that a character played by Deborah Kerr should die after she commits adultery. What was the film in question?

9. Who was Karl Struss?

10. Who dubbed Rita Hayworth's singing in the movie *Cover Girl*?

11. Can you identify Douglas Trumbell?

12. In what area did Gilbert Adrian make his mark in Hollywood circles?

13. Although Alan Jay Lerner wrote the screenplay for his musical comedy *Paint Your Wagon,* he based his work upon an adaptation by what well-known stage, screen, and television writer?

14. The film *Come Blow Your Horn* was based upon a stage play by Neil Simon and stars Frank Sinatra. What well-known television producer wrote the screenplay?

15. In his 1953 film *The Moon Is Blue,* director Otto Preminger refused to delete a certain word from his film. Thus, his film was denied the Production seal and was awarded a "C" rating by the Legion of Decency. What word caused all the problems?

16. What great comedian and clown supplied the voice for the Mad Hatter in Walt Disney's 1951 animated version of *Alice in Wonderland*?

17. In the film version of *The Solid Gold Cadillac,* what noted radio, television, and motion picture performer provided the off-screen narration?

18. In the full-length animated film *Charlotte's Web* (based on E. B. White's classic), what noted singer and film performer provided the voice for Charlotte?

19. What noted television personality once provided the singing voice for Prince Charming in Walt Disney's *Cinderella*?

ANSWERS

1. *All three supplied the voices for Mickey Mouse. Walt Disney was Mickey's voice for the first nineteen years. Jim Macdonald, who was Disney's Sound Effects Man, did Mickey's voice for nearly thirty years. Wayne Allwine supplied Mickey's voice for* Mickey's Christmas Carol.

2. *Bing Crosby.*

3. *Metropolitan baritone Robert McFerrin sang Porgy. Adele Addision did the singing for Dorothy Dandridge's Bess.*

4. *The film is one of Lloyd's most famous:* Safety Last. *Lloyd hired circus acrobat Paul Wenzel to perform stunts first so that camera angles could be set up. Wenzel, in fact, appears once in the film. He can be seen swinging from one building to another from a rope tied to his ankle—a stunt that Lloyd decided was best left to a circus performer.*

5. *Chill Wills, of all people.*

6. *Chill Wills, who also supplied the voice for television's Mr. Ed.*

7. *Mario Lanza sings the Sigmund Romberg songs.*

8. *The Legion of Decency took offense to adultery in the film* Tea and Sympathy *(1956).*

9. *Karl Struss, who died in 1981 at the age of ninety-five, won an Academy Award for his cinematography on the film* Sunrise *(1929). He also developed a soft-focus photographic lens.*

10. *Martha Mears dubbed Rita Hayworth's singing in* Cover Girl; *Anita Ellis dubbed Ms. Hayworth's singing in* The Lady From Shanghai.

11. *He was the special effects director for* Close Encounters of the Third Kind *and for* 2001: A Space Odyssey.

12. *Gilbert Adrian was a leading clothing and costume designer for numerous Hollywood stars. Rudolph Valentino's wife Natacha Rambova brought him from New York City to design her husband's clothes, and he became the costume designer for many films. He once said of Tullulah Bankhead, "She can wear more silver fox than any other woman and still look undressed." In 1939 Gilbert Adrian married Janet Gaynor.*

13. *Paddy Chayevsky did the adaptation.*

14. *Norman Lear, producer of* All in the Family *and many other shows. Years before* Come Blow Your Horn, *Norman Lear managed to get Danny Thomas's phone number and telephoned the comedian to sell him some material. Thomas asked Lear to come right over, but Lear begged off, citing important business; Lear hadn't written the material yet.*

15. *The censors didn't want audiences to hear the word "virgin." They also frowned on the word "mistress."*

16. *Ed Wynn, "the Perfect Fool."*

17. *George Burns.*

18. *Debbie Reynolds provided Charlotte's voice.*

19. *Mike Douglas.*

FREEZE FRAME

General Quiz #4

1. Oz is a famous city, but a man named Frank Oz played what role in *Star Wars* (1981)?

2. On the night of her death—July 8, 1967—all the theaters in the West End of London extinguished all their exterior lights for an hour to mourn this distinguished stage and motion-picture star. Who?

3. At age sixteen, he was arrested for vagrancy and sent to a Georgia chain gang for six days. In 1939, he wrote an oratorio that was produced by Orson Welles and performed at the Hollywood Bowl. Who is this movie star?

4. Below are listed four famous characters in Hollywood films. Can you identify in which films the characters appear and who play them?
   a. Rosa Klebb
   b. Midge Kelly
   c. Robert E. Lee Prewitt
   d. Sister Sharon Falconer

5. For circus fans: Minor Watson plays John Ringling North in what film? John Ringling North portrays himself in what film?

6. When it was released, *Time* magazine called this film "just possibly the dirtiest American picture ever legally exhibited." What film (based upon a play) was so castigated?

7. Luz Benedict the Second, Angel Obregon the Third, Jordan Benedict the Third, and Angel Obregon the First are all characters in what noted American film?

8. In what 1962 film about film-makers (starring Kirk Douglas) do people in the film study excerpts from the 1952 film about film-makers, *The Bad and the Beautiful* (also starring Kirk Douglas)?

9. The 1951 film *He Ran All the Way* was the final film appearance of what film star?

10. Judy Garland sings the "Trolley Song" in which of her films?

11. What was the first film in the history of motion pictures to gross over 100 million dollars?

12. Gene Kelly directed Jackie Gleason in a film based upon a story conceived by Jackie Gleason. Jackie Gleason also composed the music to the film. What is the film's title?

13. Who sings an aria from the opera *Samson and Delilah* in the 1935 film *Goin' to Town*?

14. Only two civilians were awarded the Bronze Star for their services in World War II. One was the great reporter Ernie Pyle. The second was a great film comedian. Who?

15. Can you name the seven dwarfs from Walt Disney's *Snow White and the Seven Dwarfs* (1937)?

16. What mistake did D. W. Griffith make in his film *Edgar Allen Poe*?

17. Sal Mineo plays a character named Red Shirt and Gilbert Roland plays Dull Knife in what John Ford western? Noble Johnson plays a character named Red Shirt in what other Ford film?

18. The musical score to what Stanley Kramer film helped make "Waltzing Mathilda" a hit tune in the United States?

ANSWERS

1. *Frank Oz plays Yoda. He also plays the corrections officer in* The Blues Brothers *(1981).*

2. *The theaters in the West End of London extinguished their lights to mourn the death of Vivien Leigh.*

3. *Robert Mitchum.*

4. a. *Rosa Klebb is played by Lotte Lenya in* From Russia With Love *(1964).*
b. *Midge Kelly is played by Kirk Douglas in* Champion *(1949).*
c. *Robert E. Lee Prewitt is played by Montgomery Clift in* From Here to Eternity *(1953).*
d. *Sister Sharon Falconer is played by Jean Simmons in* Elmer Gantry *(1960).*

5. *Minor Watson plays John Ringling North in* Trapeze *(1956). John Ringling North can be seen in* The Greatest Show on Earth *(1952).*

6. Baby Doll *(1956) based upon the controversial play by Tennessee Williams and starring Carroll Baker, caused* Time *to give out cries of outrage.*

7. *They are all characters in the George Stevens film* Giant.

8. *The film is* Two Weeks in Another Town.

9. He Ran All the Way *marked the final screen appearance of John Garfield.*

10. *Judy Garland sings the "Trolley Song" in* Meet Me in St. Louis *(1944).*

11. Jaws *(1975) was the first film to gross 100 million dollars.*

12. Gigot *(1962).*

13. *Mae West sings opera in that film.*

14. *Joe E. Brown. After the death of his son, Captain Donald Evans Brown (who died in a plane crash at the start of the war), Joe E. Brown devoted most of his energies to entertaining the troops.*

15. *The names of the seven dwarfs are: Bashful, Doc, Grumpy, Happy, Sleepy, Sneezy, and Dopey.*

16. *D. W. Griffith misspelled Poe's middle name. The title should have read:* Edgar Allan Poe.

17. *Red Shirt and Dull Knife are characters in* Cheyenne Autumn *(1964). Red Shirt is also a character in* She Wore a Yellow Ribbon.

18. *"Waltzing Mathilda" can be heard on the sound track to* On the Beach *(1959). The film was based upon the novel by Nevil Shute and starred Gregory Peck and Ava Gardner.*

FADE OUT

Relatively
Speaking

1. Cecil B. De Mille's adopted daughter Katherine plays a role in what 1947 film directed by her father?

2. On December 20, 1931, a leading actor and matinee idol died on the set of the film *Miracle Man*. Almost twenty-seven years later, on November 15, 1958, that actor's son (also a Hollywood star) died on the set of *Solomon and Sheba*. Identify both father and son.

3. In what films directed by Alfred Hitchcock can viewers see Hitchcock's daughter Patricia on the screen?

4. Everybody knows Cecil B. De Mille. Who was William De Mille?

5. Ethel, John, and Lionel Barrymore appear together in only one film. Can you name the film?

6. The son of a noted movie star plays the role of a German refugee in the Alfred Hitchcock film *Torn Curtain*. Who is he?

7. What film actor was a grand-nephew of the president of the South African Republic (during the Boer War years)?

8. What well-known actor (who appears in numerous John Ford films) was directed by his own son in the 1957 film *The Abductors*?

9. Raoul Walsh, the director, is well-known to filmgoers, but who was George Walsh?

10. In what film does the godson of Noel Coward play Noel Coward?

11. Who is Joan Fontaine's older sister?

12. The Danish-born writer-director of *Angry Red Planet* (1959) and *Reptilicus* is the son of a famous opera tenor who can be seen in such films as *Thrill of a Romance* (1945) and *Two Sisters From Boston* (1946). Can you identify the father and the son?

13. Who is Ingo Preminger?

14. The son produced such films as *Compulsion* (1959) and *The Chapman Report* (1962). The father started writing stories for Rin-Tin-Tin movies and was vice-president in charge of production at Twentieth Century Fox. Who is the father? Who is the son?

15. If you are an Errol Flynn fan and/or a Mark Twain fan, then you might be able to identify Billy and Bobby Mauch. Who are they?

16. The son of what stage-and-screen star played his father when his father's life story was brought to the screen?

17. They were three brothers. One founded London Films and directed (among other films) *The Private Life of Henry VIII* (1933). The second brother created the sets for the above-mentioned film. He also created sets for *The Thief of Baghdad.* The third brother directed (among other films) *Cry the Beloved Country.* Who were they?

18. In *Topper* (1937), this actress plays a ghost. That same year the actress's sister (also a movie star) appeared in *Vogues of 1938.* These sisters appeared separately in many, many films. Who are they?

19. The brother of a world-famous film star (associated with a band called the Bobcats) can be seen in such movies as *The Singing Sheriff, Sis Hopkins,* and *Rookies on Parade.* Who is he?

20. One brother played Diamond Pete Montana in *Little Caesar* and directed *The Sea Wolf;* another brother directed. *Across the Plains* and produced the westerns of William S. Hart; a third brother co-starred in *Madame Sphinx* and can be seen in *Pride of the Yankees* and *The Paradine Case.* Who are they?

21. In what film does Charlie Chaplin's son Michael play a scene with his father? Michael, eleven years old at the time, plays a child prodigy whose parents are former Communists.

22. The son of Keenan Wynn and the grandson of Ed Wynn is a noted scriptwriter. He wrote the script of the 1974 Burt Reynolds film *The Longest Yard.* Who is he?

23. Film star June Havoc's sister can be seen in the 1952 film *Babes of Baghdad* (and other films). June Havoc's sister also wrote a number of books. Who is she?

24. This comedian appears in such films as *McLintock* (1967) and *The Courtship of Eddie's Father* (1963). His more famous brother appears in *Cold Turkey* (1971) and *Chitty Chitty Bang Bang* (1968). Who are they?

25. Carole Lombard had a cousin who was one of the great Hollywood film directors. Who was he?

ANSWERS

1. *Cecil B. De Mille's adopted daughter Katherine plays the part of Hannah in* Unconquered.

2. *The father was Tyrone Power, Sr. The son was Tyrone Power, Jr.*

3. *Patricia Hitchcock can be seen in* Stage Fright, Strangers on a Train *(where she plays Barbara Morton), and* Psycho.

4. *William De Mille was Cecil's older brother and a film director in his own right. As opposed to Cecil's moralistic extravaganzas, William De Mille concentrated on intimate stories of gentle emotional power. His films, unfortunately, are lost.*

5. *John, Ethel, and Lionel can be seen together in* Rasputin and the Empress *(1932).*

6. *Peter Lorre, Jr., son of Peter Lorre and hs first wife Alma Weigand.*

7. *Otto Kruger. His great-uncle was Oom Paul Kruger. Otto Kruger's last film appearance was in the 1964 movie,* Sex and the Single Girl.

8. *Victor McLagen, who plays Sergeant Quincannon so well in John Ford's cavalry trilogy, was directed by Andrew V. McLagen in* The Abductors.

9. *George Walsh, Raoul's brother, was a well-known movie actor. He was originally cast to play the part of Ben Hur in the famed silent film version, but he was replaced. Raoul Walsh directed his brother in the 1916 Fox film* Blue Blood and Red. *Most of George Walsh's films are lost, however, because of a fire in the Fox studio's film vaults.*

10. *Daniel Massey (godson of Noel Coward) plays Noel Coward in* Star! *(1968), the film biography of Gertrude Lawrence.*

11. *Olivia de Havilland, who was born in Tokyo in 1916, is the sister of Joan Fontaine.*

12. *Lauritz Melchior is the father. His son Ib Melchior is the writer-producer.*

13. *Ingo Preminger, the producer of* M*A*S*H *(1970) is the brother of director Otto Preminger.*

14. *Richard Zanuck produced* Compulsion *and many other films. His father was Darryl F. Zanuck.*

15. *Billy and Bobby Mauch are the identical twin brothers (born in 1925) who play the roles of the Prince and the Pauper in the 1937 Errol Flynn film based upon Mark Twain's novel.*

16. *Will Rogers, Jr. portrays his father in* The Will Rogers Story *(1972).*

17. *These are the fabulous Korda brothers. Alexander Korda founded the London Company; Vincent Korda designed sets; Zoltan Korda directed* Cry the Beloved Country.

18. *Constance and Joan Bennett.*

19. *Bob Crosby, Bing's brother.* The Singing Sheriff *was shot in ten days, and Bob Crosby claimed that "it set back western movies exactly three years."*

20. *These three brothers are Ralph, Thomas, and John Ince.*

21. A King in New York. *The film was released in Europe in 1957, but it didn't open in the United States until 1972.*

22. *Tracy Keenan Wynn.*

23. *June Havoc's sister was the well-known striptease artist Gypsy Rose Lee. The musical* Gypsy *was based upon her life. Ms. Lee also wrote a mystery book called* The G-string Murders. *When Gypsy and her sister were quite young, they appeared together on stage in* Dancing June and Her Newsboy Songsters.

24. *Jerry Van Dyke and Dick Van Dyke.*

25. *Howard Hawks. He directed* Sergeant York, Gentlemen Prefer Blondes, Hatari!, Rio Lobo, *and many, many other films.*

Off the Set

1. As a child, the nickname for this future actress was 'Keta' because that was the way—when she was very little—she would pronounce her own first name. Can you identify this all-time screen great?

2. This singing star had two French poodles named "Your Time" and "My Time." Who was he?

3. What Hollywood actress received some press coverage from the fact that she used to dye the hair of her pet poodles to match whatever color hair she had at the time?

4. What Broadway and motion-picture actress was nicknamed by her brother "Big Easel"?

5. Press agents loved to claim that this blonde beauty queen was once the "ping-pong" champ of Europe and that ping-pong was her favorite indoor sport. Who's the actress?

6. What great singer was preparing to work in the first 3-D movie when he died on October 23, 1950?

7. What actor, by way of a practical joke, placed a dead snake in Olivia De Havilland's panties?

8. In 1928, what motion picture great took out a full-page advertisement in *Variety* to praise "The Greatest Comedy Ever Made"? The ad went on to say, "If a greater [comedy] is ever made, Chaplin will make it. Dem's my sentiments. Boy, wait till you see it!" What comedy was being praised to the skies?

9. What film and television star was world skeet champion at age sixteen?

10. What movie actress graced the first cover of *People* magazine when the magazine made its debut on March 4, 1974?

11. Can you name Cary Grant's five wives?

12. What director of more than four hundred films once gave this advice to young directors: "Be sincere. Don't be tricky. And surround yourself with good people." (Hint: he died in 1982 at the age of ninety-six.)

13. What film actor, after visiting Russia, smuggled out (in the lining of his coat) rolls of film and a spool of tape for the dancers Valery and Galina Panov?

14. A young man named Maurice Joseph Mickelwhite supposedly took his screen name from the title of a film that starred Humphrey Bogart. Can you identify him by his well-known name?

15. What all-time film great began his acting career as a female impersonator in a play called *Every Sailor* (1920)?

16. In 1948, what noted film actor got involved in a well-publicized scandal when he was arrested and charged with possession of marijuana cigarettes?

17. At a testimonial dinner held for this film star in January 1961 at the Friar's Club, poet Carl Sandburg called him "one of the most beloved illiterates this country has ever known." To whom was the poet referring?

18. What great film comedian was missing the thumb and index finger of his right hand?

19. What great film comedian once served as an understudy to Charlie Chaplin when Chaplin was a performer in Fred Karno's London Comedians?

20. Numerous film stars were forbidden by their contracts to make recordings, so this star once made a record for Columbia under the pseudonym Ruth Haig. She sang "I

Can't Begin to Tell You" from the film *The Dolly Sisters*.
Who was the actress? With what orchestra did she record
the number?

ANSWERS

1. *Greta Garbo. She once claimed that she never said, "I want to be alone." She said that she had said, " 'I want to be let alone.' There is all the difference."*

2. *Rudy Vallee, famous for "My Time Is Your Time."*

3. *Gloria De Haven.*

4. *Ethel Barrymore was called that by John Barrymore and his friend James Montgomery Flagg.*

5. *Zsa Zsa Gabor. All right, maybe ping-pong was only her second-favorite indoor sport.*

6. *Al Jolson. He was born Asa Yoelson in St. Petersburg, Russia.*

7. *That poor joke was done by Errol Flynn.*

8. *The ad was taken out by Al Jolson. The movie he praised is* The Circus.

9. *Robert Stack. He was elected to the Skeet-shooting Hall of Fame in 1971.*

10. *Mia Farrow. That first issue sold for thirty-five cents.*

11. *Cary Grant's five wives: Woolworth heiress Barbara Hutton, Virginia Cherrill, Betsy Drake, Dyan Cannon, and Barbara Harris. Barbara Harris, by the way, is not the actress, but a former publicist for a London hotel.*

12. *Allan Dwan.* Brewster's Millions *and* Getting Gertie's Garter *are just two of the better-known films he directed.*

13. *Ben Cross. He played Olympic runner Harold Abrahams in the Academy-Award-winning film* Chariots of Fire *(1982).*

14. *Michael Caine. The film, of course, was* The Caine Mutiny.

15. *James Cagney.*

16. *Robert Mitchum. He was sentenced to sixty days in Los Angeles County Jail.*

17. *Carl Sandburg was referring to Gary Cooper.*

18. *Harold Lloyd. Off-screen he wore gloves. On screen, he used latex to fake the missing fingers. His handicap, of course, did not interfere with his ability to perform incredible athletic stunts for his films.*

19. *Stan Laurel.*

20. *Betty Grable recorded the song with the Harry James Orchestra. Eventually the song was reissued under her own name.*

The Academy Awards

1. The movies' first real western hero was awarded a special Academy Award in 1957 for his "contribution to the development of the narrative film and the emergence of the screen hero." Who was he?

2. In the history of the Academy Award ceremonies, what actor was nominated most as Best Actor?

3. In 1928 Academy Awards were presented for the first time. In that first year, Academy members nominated three actors who "gave the best performance in acting, with special reference to character portrayal and effectiveness of dramatic or comedy rendition." Two of those actors were nominated for roles they portrayed in more than one film. Can you name the three actors nominated in 1928?

4. In 1942, the Academy Award ceremonies were held in the Biltmore Hotel. There was no one special emcee that year, but there was a featured speaker—a very important politician. Who was he?

5. What world-famous entertainer was presented with the only *wooden* Oscar? He received it as a special Academy Award in 1937.

6. It sometimes happens in the history of Academy Award presentations that the film that receives the award for Best Picture receives Academy Awards in no other categories (editing, writing, directing, etc.). Three films have suffered such a fate. Can you name any two of them?

7. Can you name three persons who have refused to accept their Academy Awards after having won them?

8. In 1938, what actress was nominated for an Academy Award as Best Actress for her performance in one film and for Best Supporting Actress for her performance in a different film?

9. In 1939, the twelfth year of Academy Award presentations, *Gone With the Wind* won the Oscar for Best Picture. *GWTW* (as it is affectionately abbreviated) beat out such fine films as *The Wizard of Oz, Stagecoach,* and *Wuthering Heights.* Can you name any of the other films that were nominated that year for Best Picture?

10. What actor won an Oscar in his very first film appearance, turned down a number of subsequent film offers, and was not in films again?

11. Can you identify Sacheen Littlefeather?

12. What actor was on the screen for less than ten minutes, and yet his performance was so memorable that he was nominated as Best Supporting Actor? The film was *Lust for Life* (1956).

13. Which Academy Award did Hugo Friedhofer win in 1946?

14. Not many stunt men have received Academy Awards, but in 1966, an honorary Oscar was presented to what stunt man "for achievements as a stunt man and for developing safety devices to protect stunt men everywhere"? Who received that award?

15. In 1938 an actor and an actress received honorary Academy Awards "for their significant contribution in bringing to the screen the spirit and personification of youth." Who were the young man and the young woman who received those awards?

16. In 1956 the Academy Awards officially established an

award for Best Foreign Language Film (before 1956, the Academy Board of Governors presented honorary Oscars to Foreign Language Films). What was the first movie to recieve an Oscar in the new category?

17. In 1960 Billy Wilder took home three Oscars for his work on a single picture. What was the film? What Oscars did Billy Wilder win?

18. In 1977, what well-known screen star received four Academy Award nominations? He received the nominations for his work on a single film; what was the film?

ANSWERS

1. *Bronco Billy Anderson. His real name was Max Aronson, and he was the first movie star to form his own production company. He named his company Essenay after the initial of his partner (Charles Spoor) and his own initial A ("S and A"). Clint Eastwood starred in a 1981 film called* Bronco Billy.

2. *Spencer Tracy, of course. He was nominated nine times. He won twice—in 1937 and in 1938.*

3. *Richard Barthelmess was nominated for his roles in* The Noose *and* The Patent Leather Kid. *Charles Chaplin was nominated for his role in* The Circus. *Emil Jannings was nominated for his roles in* The Last Command *and* The Way of All Flesh.

4. *Wendell Wilkie.*

5. *Edgar Bergen. The wooden statuette was a tribute to the wooden Charlie McCarthy.*

6. *The three films were* Wings *(1927/28),* Grand Hotel *(1931/32); and* Mutiny on the Bounty *(1935).*

7. *Dudley Nichols, Marlon Brando, and George C. Scott.*

8. *Fay Bainter. She was nominated as Best Actress for* White Banners *and as Best Supporting Actress for* Jezebel. *She won the Oscar that year for Best Supporting Actress.*

9. *Other films nominated in 1939 were* Good-bye, Mr. Chips; Dark Victory; Love Affair; Mr. Smith Goes to Washington; *and* Of Mice and Men. *Now the Best Picture category is limited to five films.*

10. *Harold Russell. This handicapped veteran of World War II had lost both hands and won an Academy Award for his moving performance in William Wyler's* The Best Years of Our Lives.

11. *At the 1973 Academy Awards ceremony, Sacheen Littlefeather was the Apache woman who told the audience that Marlon Brando would not accept his Oscar for Best Actor because of the way American films had portrayed the American Indian.*

12. *Anthony Quinn.*

13. *Hugo Friedhofer won a 1946 Oscar for his score to* The Best Years of Our Lives. *He was nominated throughout the years for eight more Oscars.*

14. *Yakima Canutt. For the film* Stagecoach, *for example, he was the second unit director.*

15. *Mickey Rooney and Deanna Durbin were the personification of youth to the Academy.*

16. La Strada, *produced by Dino De Laurentis and Carlo Ponti, and directed by Federico Fellini, was the first film to win in the best foreign-language film category.*

17. *Billy Wilder won three Oscars for his work on* The Apartment. *He received Academy Awards as Best Producer, Best Director, and he shared the screenwriting award with his co-author I. A. L. Diamond.*

18. *In 1977 Woody Allen received four Academy Award nominations for his work on* Annie Hall. *He was nominated in the categories of Best Producer, Best Actor, Best Director, and author of Best Screenplay (with his co-author Marshall Brickman). He won the awards for directing and screenplay writing.* Annie Hall *was voted Best Picture.*